# PERMISSION SLIPS

# PERMISSION SLIPS

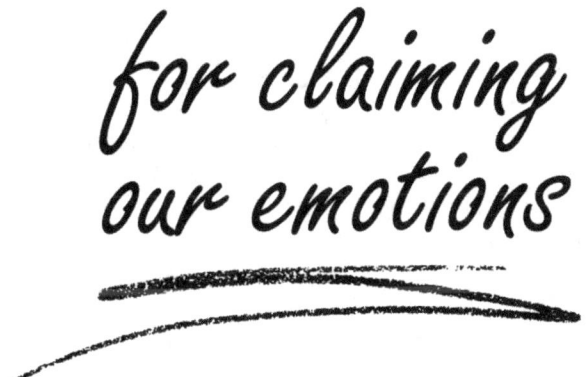
*for claiming our emotions*

An emotional resilience project
by the **Courageous Hearts Collective**

Copyright © 2025 Courageous Hearts Collective

All rights reserved. No part of this publication may be reproduced, distributed or transmitted in any form or by any means without permission of the publisher, except in the case of brief quotations referencing the body of work and in accordance with copyright law.

The information given in this book should not be treated as a substitute for professional medical advice; always consult a medical practitioner. Any use of information in this book is at the reader's discretion and risk. Neither the author nor the publisher can be held responsible for any loss, claim or damage arising out of the use, or misuse, of the suggestions made, the failure to take medical advice or for any material on third party websites.

ISBN 978-1-916529-36-6 Paperback
ISBN 978-1-916529-37-3 Ebook

The Unbound Press
www.theunboundpress.com

Hey unbound one!

Welcome to this magical book brought to you by The Unbound Press.

At The Unbound Press we believe that when women write freely from the fullest expression of who they are, it can't help but activate a feeling of deep connection and transformation in others. When we come together, we become more and we're changing the world, one book at a time!

This book has been carefully crafted by both the contributors and publisher with the intention of inspiring you to move ever more deeply into who you truly are.

We hope that this book helps you to connect with your Unbound Self and that you feel called to pass it on to others who want to live a more fully expressed life.

With much love,

Nicola Humber

Founder of The Unbound Press

www.theunboundpress.com

# Contents

| | |
|---|---|
| Acknowledgements | ix |
| Permission to matter | 1 |
| You're invited to join us on a courageous journey | 5 |
| The Emotional Check-In | 11 |
| Your Emotional Starting Point | 14 |
| Permission to validate your emotional experience | 17 |
| Permission to sit in chaos with your emotions | 25 |
| Permission to feel fear | 33 |
| Permission to see your emotions as gifts | 39 |
| Permission to nurture yourself with compassion | 45 |
| Permission to love yourself and all your parts | 55 |
| Permission to know that you're enough | 71 |
| Permission to fall apart | 81 |
| Permission to be vulnerable | 93 |
| Permission to feel "bad" emotions | 105 |
| Permission to let it rip | 111 |
| Permission to feel shame | 119 |
| Permission to be perfectly imperfect | 129 |
| Permission to love imperfectly | 135 |
| Permission to choose love | 147 |
| Permission to give yourself what you needed when you were young | 153 |
| Permission to not know | 159 |
| Permission to choose | 163 |
| Permission to claim self-authority | 175 |
| Permission to show yourself grace and compassion | 179 |
| Permission to trust the sacred | 183 |
| Permission to heal | 189 |

| | |
|---|---|
| Permission to heal collective wounds | 195 |
| Permission to have a courageous heart | 201 |
| Permission to celebrate | 205 |
| Permission to be on a journey of becoming | 209 |
| Permission to change the cultural narrative around emotions | 215 |
| Who We Are and How We Got Here | 223 |
| Closing Thoughts | 233 |
| Invitation to write a letter to yourself | 235 |
| A Call to Community | 237 |
| Permission to receive support on your journey from here | 239 |
| Permission Slips for Your Emotions | 241 |
| Resources for Further Exploration | 259 |
| Index by Author | 263 |

# Acknowledgments

**For all the courageous hearts seeking a brave space to feel their emotions fully.**

The selections in this book are just a sliver of what came forth when we claimed our self-authority and gave ourselves permission to identify and engage with our emotions in a conscious and loving way.

Our intention is that by sharing our stories and poems of emotional alchemy, you may find it possible to expand beyond wounded patterns of reacting and reconnect with your divine essence.

We are grateful that you have picked up this book, and we honor your desire to learn how your emotions can serve you and those around you.

**For those who came before us, we honor the lessons you taught us.**

We offer our greatest thanks to the Emotionally Fit Leaders Team – Angela Trainor, Carol Ross, Irv Kooris, and Justine Williams (emotionallyfitleaders.com) – who first brought the writers of this book together in a course on mastering emotional resilience. We are also deeply grateful to Leza Danly, Jeanine Mancusi, and Michelle Goss, whose Great Story coaching programs informed and impacted us in powerful ways.

We have deep gratitude for our other teachers, mentors, colleagues, family, and friends who have supported us along our own journeys.

Finally, we are deeply grateful for the grace that helps each of us grow and find a sense of emotional completeness, self-worth, self-authority, and loving acceptance of what is, within ourselves and others.

With love,

*Deborah, Holly, Maggie, Marna, and Owen*
The Courageous Hearts Collective

# Permission to matter

## Emotions Matter

*by Owen Sea Luckey*

Today you are being heard in a new way
through this collective group of
fierce Women Warriors
on a quest to normalize and experience
all our emotions.

Yes, I feel your fear and excitement
vibrating as you put pen to page.

Your compassion and passion
for the newness of this shared space
and the wisdom that holds us.

You are the voice of your soul's essence
and many generations.
The one who has chosen not to repeat patterns
of emotions so deep
and so painful it has cost her
and created her.

The emotions that now get named
not glued like glitter scattered
on a blank page.
Beautiful, messy,
sometimes sticky
can be shifted by the slightest breeze.

It's with this awareness of
all our emotions
and witnessing them
we have come to share our maps to seeing,
being, and healing
each other and you.

I am here to say, don't stay silent,
breathe into your voice,
don't stay silent.

The quiet one who lives loudly within.
Step out!
We have you.

This comes as an expansion of
your language of emotions –
feel and express
your full range.

I am here to tell you,
I/we have you!
We love you!
You MATTER!!

Your emotions matter,
naming them matters,
being witnessed in them matters.

Bring on the ease, grace, love
and the darkest flames of rage!
It MATTERS!!

The passion, love, and violence boiling!
It matters!

The seen and not heard,
I want to hear from you!
It MATTERS!

Together we can surf this ocean of emotions
and flow with the tides and waves.
Breathe.

# You're invited to join us on a courageous journey

## Welcome!

Through this book, we invite you into an emotional resiliency circle, where you can experience a greater depth and range of emotions.

By sharing our experiences of emotional alchemy, we are motivated by a desire to offer insights and inspiration to anyone who is curious about exploring this sensitive and potent aspect of being human.

In choosing this book, you may be longing to stop getting hijacked by your emotions and to create a more helpful relationship with them. You may be wishing for a deeper connection with yourself and others. And, you may be willing to take courageous steps forward in service of this – because the cost of denying your emotions and feeling alone is becoming too painful.

The process of feeling all our emotions takes courage, and it doesn't always feel good or comfortable.

But this isn't a journey to feeling good or comfortable all the time. It's a journey to feeling more alive, whole, and free.

Feeling all our emotions is how we cultivate resilience. While our culture would have us believe that resilience means pushing our emotions aside and "soldiering on," we believe resilience actually develops from intentionally allowing ourselves to experience our emotions and come out the other side. Being in flow with our emotions allows us to accept and dance with reality in a more helpful way and create a more positive culture within ourselves and the society we are collectively creating.

Feeling all our emotions is a necessary first step in taking responsibility for our lives – that is, claiming the power to choose our responses.

## Who We Are

We thought you might like to know something about how the Courageous Hearts Collective came to be and how we came to write this book.

The five of us met in the Fall of 2020, when we participated in an advanced coaching program led by Emotionally Fit Leaders that focused on fostering emotional resilience in ourselves and our clients. That course became a gateway to a deeper understanding of, and connection to, our emotions and ourselves.

As coaches, we support people on their journeys from where they are now, to where they wish to be. We noticed, while working with our clients, that engaging more deeply with their emotions was an essential step in this journey. By focusing on what they're experiencing internally in the moment, clients learn to navigate through the chaos and confusion that often accompany change, using their emotions as stepping stones toward forward motion and lasting change.

We knew we needed to become more humble and courageous in processing our own emotions so we could guide our clients through this process. We learned that by denying our feelings, as emotional coach Nijiama Smalls writes, "we lose the ability to see the good in situations and people, enjoy the simple moments, persevere through conflict, and bring our best selves to all of our relationships." By expanding the range of emotions that we could notice, name, and accept within ourselves, we expanded our ability to respond to whatever came up and to model this process for others.

When the course ended in early 2021, five of us continued to meet weekly to further our exploration of our emotional terrains. Sharing our emotional experiences through conversation and writing, we witnessed one another with deep compassion and an appreciation that whatever we were feeling in the moment was perfect and just right.

**The growth edge for all of us has been to expand into the experience of our emotions and give a back seat to our stories.**

To be clear, we're not saying stories aren't important. As writer Maya Angelou says, "There is no greater agony than an untold story inside of you." Your truth matters. Stories are real and present; they are through-lines to our lives, and we use them to create meaning from our experiences. And yet, the emotions contained within the stories are what need our attention and care.

In this book, we share some of the stories and poems that allowed us to access our raw emotions and to heal.

This process of being with all of our emotions has not been smooth sailing for any of us – we all experienced the pandemic amidst full lives, with mess and magic. Through regular two-hour calls, we have grown comfortable sharing the edgiest and most tender parts of our being with one another. This practice of sharing and writing has fostered safety, intimacy, and a deep sense of emotional acceptance. We have grown our emotional capacity and wisdom, expanded beyond our wounded patterns of reacting, and transformed our relationships with ourselves and others.

Our rich discussions ignited a passion and commitment to share our journeys and insights through a collaborative book. We span a wide range of ages, time zones, and life experiences. Holly McLoughlin is in the UK, Marna Fujimoto-Pihl is in Canada, and Owen Sea Luckey, Maggie Pierce, and Deborah Thornton are in the US. While some of us were acquainted before we came together, at the time of this writing, we have never met in person as a group!

Thank you for joining us on our resilience journey and braving new territories with us as we navigate the emotional landscapes of life.

## Our Invitation

We invite you to join the five of us on a journey to greater resilience, wholeness, and response-ability. We have created a brave space that also serves as a temple of celebration for each other's grace, passions, and gifts.

You, dear reader, are the sixth member of our emotional resilience circle. We are delighted you are here with us, as we share our hearts and the wisdom born through our diverse experiences.

The pieces we share in this book explore the emotional landscapes of our lives, painted beautifully in our own unique patterns and textures. Our intention is to share some glimpses of how we experience and relate to our emotions, so they may serve as a resource for your own journey toward a more authentic and expansive emotional life.

We invite you to explore the emotional landscapes within these pages alongside us and to begin to reflect on your own landscape, knowing that you are loved, accepted, and recognized for your brilliant nature and your radiant heart.

## How This Book Works

As we began sharing our poems and stories, we recognized that some of the most painful parts of our journeys were linked to emotions we had been told to hide or dismiss. In giving ourselves permission to have those emotions, opportunities for healing and growth emerged.

We found that flipping our internal script from "I'm not allowed to" or "I shouldn't" to "I can" or "I get to" had a powerful impact on our individual evolution. By granting ourselves permission to experience our emotions in a conscious and loving way, we began to take back our power and reclaim our self-authority and wholeness. This experience led us to organize the book's sections around the concept of permission slips – those powerful pieces of paper that opened or closed the door to us as children.

Most of the pieces in this book include a list of emotions the author experienced when she was writing. We invite you to notice what emotions are present for you while reading each piece, holding compassion and curiosity for both the writer and yourself.

At the end of each section, we offer a space for you to pause, check in with your emotions, reflect on the themes in the pieces you just read, and notice the permission slips you want to give yourself to expand your emotional range. Again, we invite you to hold compassion and curiosity for whatever shows up for you. There are no right or wrong answers here – what you notice in the moment is perfect and just right for where you are on your journey.

The book culminates with an invitation to write an emotionally nurturing letter to a part of yourself that needs your loving attention.

You may notice that sometimes we capitalize emotions or parts of ourselves, and other times we don't. When you see something capitalized (like Love, Rage, or Little One), it's a sign that the writer was experiencing a personal relationship with that emotion or part of herself.

Some sections will resonate for you more than others, and some might not speak to you at all. You might read the book cover to cover, or perhaps you'll jump right to what intuitively calls to you. Trust that however you choose to interact with this book is right for you. Feel free to highlight or underline, make notes in the book, or keep a journal. This book is meant to be a journey and a conversation.

We've also included a list of emotions at the back of the book, with permission slips to help you experience and learn from them.

## Our Agreements

We are honored to have you with us. In this circle, we create a brave space to witness the full range of our emotions – the highs and the lows, the emptiness and the richness of the messy middle – and to celebrate the gifts and joys of life.

In joining this circle, we ask that you keep your heart and mind open to what you read and experience, stay present and curious, leave judgment at the door, and hold our stories and yours with compassion, acceptance, and the grace of all that is.

This space is not intended as therapeutic. It is intended as a space for self-exploration and reflection. It's a space for finding and creating your own safety by experiencing your emotional guidance system.

It is important to let you know that some pieces in this book use strong language and express raw, unfiltered emotions, which may feel challenging to read or witness. Some pieces describe responses to traumatic experiences. We have not inserted "trigger warnings" within the book. We trust that, as a human who is naturally resourceful, creative, and whole, you will take responsibility for yourself while reading this book, pause where you need some space, and give yourself the care and support you need.

And now, onward, courageous heart!

**We invite you to turn the page and join our circle.**

# *The Emotional Check-In*

Emotions are part of our humanity, from the depths of despair to the expansiveness of love. Your emotions serve a purpose, and they matter.

Many people can name "mad," "sad," or "glad" as emotions they experience, and our culture offers us rather broad terms like "upset," "emotional," "stressed," or "off" to describe our feelings. Research by Matthew Lieberman, Daniel J. Seigel, and countless others shows that naming our emotions as precisely as possible (known as "emotional granularity") can reduce the emotion's charge and allow us to more effectively get at why it has appeared, so we can tend to it.

The practice of naming and experiencing our emotions supports our emotional and physical well-being. Expanding the range of emotions that we notice and are willing to experience (our emotional "comfort zone") can help us cultivate the resilience that is so essential in these changing and challenging times.

The five of us meet regularly on a conscious journey to explore and express our emotions. We begin every call with an emotional check-in, answering the question:

## What emotions have you been experiencing in the last 24-48 hours?

As a first step in joining our circle, we invite you to reflect on that question for yourself.

You can make a note of the emotions you have been noticing here:

If you need some inspiration to identify your emotions, you can use the *Spectrum of Emotions* below as a guide. (You can download a full-size, in-color version to print from the Resources section of our website: courageous-hearts.com.)

## THE SPECTRUM OF EMOTIONS

Love

Compassion  Joy  Happiness

Thrill  Eagerness  Excitement  Hope  Trust  Passion

Confusion  Impatience  Well-Being  Contentment  Optimism

Guilt  Sadness  Pity  Overwhelm  Worry  Doubt  Frustration

Fear  Anxiety  Angst  Anger  Fury  Resentment  Pessimism

Blame  Jealousy/Envy  Hurt  Rejection  Humiliation

Loneliness  Worthlessness  Revenge  Hatred

Hopelessness  Emptiness

Despair

---

This graphic was developed by Deborah Thornton, MSW, CPCC (https://prismatic-coaching.com). It incorporates concepts from the Tiers of Emotion (©2005, Concept Synergy) and the Resiliency Circle Cornerstones (©2021, emotionallyfitleaders.com).

# Your Emotional Starting Point

The list you just created is your starting point for exploring your emotions.

Consider the following questions:

- What came up for you when you asked yourself to recall what emotions you've been experiencing? Was there resistance? Curiosity? Thrill?

- Did you experience any numbness or blankness, like you were at a loss to name your emotions? How do you feel about that?

- For the emotions you are aware of, how do you notice or experience them? For example, do you feel them in your body? If so, where?

- Have you experienced any of the emotions you listed for longer than 24 hours? If so, which one(s)?

- What emotion(s) do you notice you feel most often?

You can make a note of your first reflections here:

# *Permission to validate your emotional experience*

**Breaking the Mold: Embracing Emotion as the New Norm**

by Holly McLoughlin

"What did you feel around your parents or caregivers when you were a child?" This query in a course by Lisa A. Romano brought a whirlwind of despair, shame, and anger at myself for being stumped. I was unable to say what I felt, and that was deeply frustrating. Here I was in a group space that was supposed to be helping me, and I couldn't even answer the first question.

My inner critic quickly geared up, letting me know what a failure I was. My wounded inner child wondered whether maybe I was too bad, too broken, too damaged to be helped. After all, this wasn't my first experience of seeking help and feeling that I didn't know the answers to what I was being asked. My wise adult self took a breath and chose to ask for some ideas to help me in the group space.

My diary from that time said:

> I became super angry with the course during the week. I identified that I missed out on the first stage of development, which gives a secure sense of bonding to mother and father (to life and the world). I realize I often feel like I can't trust the world or that things will work

*out okay for me. However, I became frustrated at not being able to tap into my feelings about that. Then I got a wonderful reply from a lady called Jenni, who said to feel what I feel now, rather than look for what I felt in the past. Ahh, unleashed! So here goes:*
*I am fucking furious that I don't feel safe, loved, accepted, enough, supported...*

This gave me the permission slip I needed to admit to myself how I currently feel about the past. That's what validating your emotional experience is. A great big permission slip to say, "This is what I feel about that. This is how I experienced it." You have a right to feel that, even if others experienced the same thing in a different way. Having different experiences from someone else doesn't have to invalidate the other's perspective.

I had longed to feel at peace in myself, because most of the time I didn't. I was, and still can be, a master at masking my vulnerabilities, so much so that most people didn't have a clue. On the outside I seemed sorted, yet on the inside I was a normal, messy human being like everyone else on the planet. I just loved to think I was the only one who was a secret weirdo. I mean, it's not like we talk about that often and openly much, is it?

Maybe you're privileged to have some safe people to get vulnerably real with, but I didn't back then. It would have freaked me out to be seen in all my real and messy glory, and I'd have run a mile from people who tried to see me for real. I'd have judged others for it too. I was terrified of exposing those parts of me that I wanted to keep in the shadows, and I expected others to do the same with their wilder parts.

Maybe, like me, you have felt the pressure to appear "okay," to wear a smile, even when your heart is aching? Said "Yes" when everything inside was screaming "No"? Held in your passion or love for fear of it being too much? Or tried to appear strong and together, when deep down inside you were afraid or were shattering?

Perhaps, like me, you've longed to just be you, and to experience more joy, happiness, or freedom? Or wished someone would actually want to know the truth when they casually ask, "How are you?" That you could tell the truth about who you are, what happened, and how you felt? Or longed to boldly celebrate how great you really are and dance with glee!

I'm sure you have, because we all have. We are all products of a cultural mold that demands we keep our emotions, especially the so-called "negative" or "intense" ones, in check. There can be days when we long to have someone be there with us, in the chaos of life and all our emotions, yet somehow it doesn't always seem safe to.

Why?

Our culture often stigmatizes the full feeling and expression of emotions, and there is an unwritten rule that many of us learn very early on:

**"It's not safe to feel my feelings."**

It can seem dangerous, improper, even shameful to feel what you do. The social environment conditions us to avoid and move away from uncomfortable feelings, rather than move towards them with acceptance and curiosity about how they are trying to guide us.

We are given messages verbally and non-verbally that lead to this, like the ones my fellow writers shared with me when I asked what messages they were given about their emotions when younger:

"If you're going to cry, go do it alone in your room."

"You're oversensitive."

"Don't cry. Try to be positive."

"Oh, you're just like your mother" [or another person], in response to sharing an emotion.

"Apologize for that emotional [passionate] outburst right now!"

And my personal favorite: the look a mother gives that freezes you in your steps.

Rarely has the process for healthy emoting been modeled. Rarely does culture tell us that all emotions are natural responses to our experiences that help you to decipher what message this pulsing energy is bringing to your attention. Nor are we commonly shown the process of noticing, thanking, feeling, and interpreting our emotions.

When feelings arise as a natural response to life, it seems as though society is invalidating them, nudging us to disconnect, isolate, hold in, numb out, minimize, substitute, exaggerate, joke or be sarcastic to cope with them. We avoid the feelings instead of allowing them to flow to completion.

The message many of us got was that emotions must be had in a socially acceptable way, but not always in a healthy way.

**You've likely been taught to keep your emotions in check, rather than to check in with what emotions you're feeling and the wisdom they're bringing you.**

The assumption is that emotions are not useful, a nuisance, are something wrong with me, do not matter, are wrong, or worthless, too big, and less than logic.

Sometimes our emotions are falsely made into our identity. The emotions you felt momentarily or as a response to your environment become associated with your personality or even who you are. For example, you're the angry one (or type), the sensitive one, the moody one, the pessimistic one, the not-enough one, the unlovable one, the overexcited one, the overly passionate one, or even the optimistic or happy-go-lucky one.

Historically, emotions have been portrayed as the opposite of being rational, as a sign of weakness, instability, or a high-risk endeavor. In the West, we learn that reason is more useful than "petty" emotions. Emotions have been unjustly cast as a barrier to rational thinking and to progress or success.

Many cultures see the expression of certain emotions, like anger or sadness, as a loss of control, a sign of personal failing. Some cultures shame people for saying no. Others can be gender based, like "big boys don't cry."

**The core message of this book is that it's time to break the old mold of emotions being a hindrance.**

**Emotions need to be cast as wisdom keepers, guiding your way through life, when you know how to let them be useful to you.**

I remember feeling overwhelmed, yet I was too ashamed to ask for help. It didn't feel safe for me. I believed that asking for support was an admission of weakness and failure. I felt it left me wide open to criticism, judgment, and negative consequences.

I thought I was afraid of what others would think, of being rejected. I have come to realize that I was afraid of the meaning I was making up about the kind of person it made me, and of not being able to love and accept myself.

Only when I finally acknowledged my feelings, when I stopped resisting my emotions and let them move freely through my body and mind, could I heed their guidance and nurture who I really am.

I needed to adapt my way of being; to slow down, take care of myself, and give myself a permission slip to feel what I felt, and then lovingly ask for what I needed. I also needed to learn how to do this by sharing my raw emotions in the safety of my fellow writers, and by observing how they processed or held compassion for the emotions I struggled with, the ones that hijacked my behavior, often against the will of my wiser self.

We don't always get what we ask for, as others have their own wounds, and because that's just life sometimes. To me, though, it feels a lot more empowering to know I can work out what I want and attempt to create it. It takes acceptance of who I really am and what I feel, without the story of what that means about me or others.

Knowing that I am a dynamic being rather than a fixed quantity, what I feel and need this week will be different to the next week, or year, or decade. It's okay not to feel okay with our experiences and the unknown, as we journey through life. You can still embrace the more blissful realms too, even in the midst of deeply constricting feelings. It took me ages to understand this paradox. I mistakenly thought I had to get rid of my bad feelings and aim to only feel the good ones.

All emotions are neutral, until we attach a story to what they mean. Despite the common story that you may drown in the depths of emotion and never get out alive, or be so shattered that the pieces will never become whole again, you can (and you will) re-emerge brighter. Most likely you have already done this a few times before. I'd bet you can think of at least one story when you were in the depths and managed to find your way through. You have access to all the inner resources you need.

Unfortunately, the consequences of our societal norms stretch beyond the individual. They seep into the very fabric of our relationships, our workplaces, our communities. When we silence our emotions to be socially acceptable, we create a society that is disconnected from its core. We neglect a vital part of our human experience. We forget that it's our emotions that connect us, that make us human, and that can heal our world.

Countless studies show this norm not only suppresses the authentic human experience; it also breeds a range of mental health issues.

When you allow your emotions to matter, you matter.

When you love and nurture your emotions, you feel more loved and supported.

It does take some courage in the early part of the journey to let down your walls and experience emotional in-to-me-see (intimacy) with yourself and with safe others.

One of my greatest breakthroughs at the start of my emotional expansion was being told that my experiencing a certain feeling doesn't invalidate what another person feels differently, or vice versa. In other words:

**Two people can go through the same experience and have wildly different feelings about it, and both people's experiences are equally valid.**

This means you can give yourself a permission slip to admit, at least to yourself in the beginning, how you really feel or felt about the things you have experienced. Guilt and shame free. You can notice and name the emotion or describe its qualities and sensations, and say, "Thank you for letting me know how that felt for me."

By embracing paradoxes like the ability to feel emotions as expansive and contracting at the same time, you can find clarity in confusion, passion in pain, beauty in the ugly, "enoughness" in the flaws. Even the uncomfortable emotions can serve you positively if you learn to let them. In other words, you can notice the gifts of your wounds and how they have shaped you for the better. You can evolve your pain and suffering into medicine. You can feel more at peace, more freedom, more self-assured by feeling through the emotional experiences you are in resistance to feeling, all the way to completion.

So, dear reader, as we navigate our lives and this book, remember that **we are all emotional beings.**

Emotions aren't a sign of weakness, but a sign of our humanity and a form of intelligence that needs to be celebrated. The invitation here is to give yourself permission to embrace the whole of the wisdom available to you, not only the socially acceptable forms, as all of it can be useful to you.

It's time to question your social norms, to give yourself a permission slip to embrace your emotions, all of them, because they make us who we are. They make us human.

### Emotions the author experienced:

Shame, fear, overwhelm, rejection, abandonment, doubt, joy, well-being, optimism, compassion, trust, peace, love, passion, contentment.

# EMOTIONAL CHECK-IN

Throughout this book you're invited to practice the emotional check-in by naming and feeling your emotions. You can refer to the *Spectrum of Emotions* earlier in the book to help you name what you feel, just as we do. Each time you practice checking in with and naming your emotions, you are building your emotional awareness and capacity. You're also invited to create permission slips in relation to your emotions. You may find inspiration from our permission slips at the back of this book.

---

What emotions do you feel in relation to validating your emotional experiences?




What beliefs do you hold about which emotions are okay to feel, when it's safe to feel them, and how you should express them?




Is there a permission slip you could give yourself in relation to validating your emotional experiences?

# *Permission to sit in chaos with your emotions*

**Diving in with Chaos**

*by Marna Fujimoto-Pihl*

There was a time when emotions felt quite chaotic to me. Being a sensitive person, I can get overstimulated easily and big feelings can sweep in quickly. I think about, feel, and process things deeply, and sometimes it can take a tremendous effort to manage those thoughts and feelings.

For decades, I worked hard to maintain the illusion of keeping it all together, of appearing calm, cool, and collected. Sometimes, I succeeded. Other times, not so much. Whenever the dam I tried so hard to contain everything behind would start to crack or would burst, I'd feel betrayed by my emotions and ashamed.

When humans experience heightened emotions like fear or anger, all rational responses can go out the window, and we may say and do things that hurt others or create feelings of disconnection. Since connection and belonging are so essential to our survival as humans, it's understandable why our instinct might be to avoid or shut down anything that seems to threaten our sense of security.

We've also had centuries of patriarchal culture telling us that intellect and reason are "right" while emotions are "wrong." We've absorbed the beliefs that emotions are untrustworthy, wild, even dangerous – and that we are weak to allow ourselves to feel them. Because of this, most of us are taught to "control" our emotions by whatever means necessary – by dismissing and ignoring them, bottling them up, pushing them down, or distracting or numbing ourselves so we don't feel them.

Emotions, however, are "energy in motion." They are meant to flow, and when we try to dam them up, they eventually "leak out sideways" in toxic ways, or they explode out. Suppressed emotions can also manifest into pain, illness, and disease. Denying ourselves our emotions is what causes the most chaos in our lives.

**In other words, the unhealthy ways we have learned to "deal with" our emotions are far more chaotic – and dangerous – than the emotions themselves.**

We wrote this book to model that emotions – and the uncomfortable, sometimes messy chaos we experience – are a normal part of being human, not something to be feared and avoided. Emotions aren't inherently bad or good, they simply are. If you experience uncomfortable, constricting, or challenging emotions, there's absolutely nothing wrong with you. You are not alone!

We also wrote this book to share the experience of sitting with the chaos of our emotions so you can see it's possible to allow and be with all of it AND come out the other side. You won't get pulled under. In fact, you'll often discover you move through the emotions faster and more completely.

Emotions are a natural physiological response to the circumstances and events of life, and life itself is full of chaos. Chaos is essential for transformation – it's where elements get broken down and rearranged into a more coherent design. Our evolution and survival therefore require us to embrace a certain amount of chaos daily.

Any time humans attempt to create change, evolve, break cycles, or rewrite the narratives, we need to go through a period of chaos first. When we buy into the lie that we must avoid chaos at all costs, we end up giving our power away for the promise of control, safety, and stability.

Our power as humans lies in our ability to choose.

And choosing to be in the chaos is in service of our greater growth as humans.

Choosing to allow our emotions to be as they are by giving ourselves space to experience them activates the observer part of ourselves, a "higher self" that can witness those emotions without being attached to the story we often make up about having them. The observing self can hold space for our feelings while we tend to the emotional need underneath. It acts like a life raft on which we can float, riding the waves until the storm passes.

Choosing to feel our emotions means that we can move from feeling helpless and scared – a victim that chaos is happening to – to an active observer who has power and agency within that chaos. You get to ride the waves of your emotions, trusting they will subside sooner than you think. And when the waves pass, you get to investigate why they showed up and appreciate the incredible intelligence of their design.

Our emotions are always pointing us in the direction of what we need and want to heal and thrive. We dive into the chaos of our emotions and feel it all, SO THAT we can gain the wisdom needed to grow and evolve as human beings.

As I began discovering that emotions play an important function in my growth and expansion as a human, and as I practiced creating space to be in flow with them, I stopped being so afraid of feeling them.

There are certainly emotions that still feel challenging or uncomfortable to experience, but I am now more willing to lean in and ride the waves until they pass. Leaning in takes courage, allowing myself to feel vulnerable takes courage, but I know it means I will be able to grow.

In the throes of my emotions, there is a choice point. For a time, I might feel myself being tossed about in the waves and I may try frantically to swim away. When I choose to surrender to the chaos, I remember I can float and ride the waves instead.

There it is.
There's a swell, the waters rise.
Don't fight it.
Stay with it,
allowing,
surrendering.
Be with,
sitting in.
Wave passes over,
and then it is gone,
and you are washed, fresh, anew.
Remnants appear before you,
like shells on a beach,
glittering in the sunlight.
They are messages
this mighty wave has left for you
to explore, to discover,
to investigate, calling you to ponder:
What was the purpose
of the wave?
What caused it?
And now that it's gone,
what do you want?
What do you need?

Waves come and go.
So do emotions.
That is a truth of life.
You can't dam up an ocean, or a river.
It's meant to flow,
meant to swell up,
then move on.

**Emotions the author experienced:**

Curiosity, relief, gratitude, trust, wonder.

## Ode to Chaos
*by Deborah Thornton*

Oh, Chaos, you great disruptor!
Interrupter
Pre-empter of the best-laid plans
Confuser
Infuser of flux and uncertainty into how things are "supposed" to go
Concealer of imagined outcomes
Revealer of myriad possibilities
Primordial stew
Swirling, unfettered pool, without boundaries, limits, rules
Infinite raw materials of all that is
Overwhelming, or exhilarating?
Trap, or springboard?
Paralysis, or momentum?
It's a matter of choice
Courage
Commitment
Trust
Hope…
Permission.

**Emotions the author experienced:**

Confusion, curiosity, hope, self-authority, freedom.

## Reflections on Chaos

*by Owen*

Chaos

Can either ignite my soul or take me down...

I have a true love/hate relationship with chaos. Chaos rises, bringing uncertainty and overwhelm. Overwhelm is my way of attempting to slow it all down, or get control.

Forgetting that if I take a breath, get still, I can be in the chaos with curiosity and spaciousness. White space, liminal space, an astronaut slowing down, viewing matter from space.

From here I can see and be with chaos, as opposed to raging against it, trying to get control of the uncontrollable.

We all live together in chaos.

Chaos is creative and vibrant, sometimes loud and musical. Chaos can be silent and obscure, and in the absence of noise, becomes sublime. When I can be with chaos, I can find what's right, a way forward, a choice bubbles up and things get real. My body is awake, I am in flow, my breath is deep and full, I can see.

When I sink into the unknown of chaos with overwhelm and fear, desperate to get control, chaos takes me down. My body becomes tense, my breath is short, my eyes don't focus on what's right, I am trying to make sense of chaos.

Chaos doesn't make sense, until it does...

I have to discern and listen from all my senses to be in it and grow forward, even when the path is foggy and dense.

This is where the magic of chaos plays in all our lives, gifting us time and space with "Ahas" and "OMG you can't make life up!"

I have grown to respect and honor chaos.

I choose not to struggle with chaos, rather use it as an opportunity to put on my explorer hat and create the map forward.

I am awake to chaos.

**Emotions the author experienced:**

Overwhelm, fear, anxiety, worry, doubt.

# EMOTIONAL CHECK-IN

What emotions do you feel in relation to sitting with chaos?

What sensations do you notice in your body when faced with chaos or the unknown?

What permission slip could you give to yourself to sit with the messiness of life?

# *Permission to feel fear*

## Forging a New Relationship with Fear

*by Marna*

There is a photo of me at two years old, standing on the mini sidewalk that extended from our old carport. I am wailing in fear. Littered on the ground all around me are catkins – those flower-bud things that fall from poplar trees and look like eerie seahorses. I was petrified of them when I was little.

I am desperate for my parents to scoop me up in the safety of their arms and carry me across this sea of alien creatures to where they are working in the shed. But apparently, my parents are so baffled and amused by this "ridiculous" phobia that they get the camera to snap a photo of me.

This actual memory is vague, but its imprint is stored in my cells. I know it is because fear can still feel like this for me at times: being paralyzed and unable to move forward … feeling small and ill-equipped to navigate the scary unknown before me … the desperation for some sort of reassurance and guidance, to be shown the way forward … and the feelings of loneliness and defeat when it doesn't come.

Of course, this one moment in time did not define how I would relate to fear for the rest of my life. It's just likely my earliest experience of being left alone to navigate it.

Fast forward seven years, and I can remember my mom telling me that I am being offered a spot in a special program. This means that every week or so, I'd be bussed to a different school and take my classes with other kids for the day. I am intimidated by all the new things I'd have to face, but mostly I feel worried about missing out on things at my current school. I'm especially anxious that my friends at my current school might decide to exclude me from their group.

I don't remember if I felt comfortable sharing my fears of missing out with my mom. I just remember her trying hard to reason with me that this was a good opportunity. In the end, though, I say no. The possibility of being excluded just feels too risky. My mom is clearly baffled and disappointed, and in that moment, I experience it as a palpable sense of her "giving up" on me.

The feeling of fear becomes associated with the pain of separation, that "withdrawing of love" feeling. As I recall it now, I feel myself shrink a little, my stomach tightens, my breathing gets a bit shallower. Back then, I was still at a loss for how to navigate the intense and overwhelming feelings of fear, and I also began to sense that something was wrong with me for feeling them.

Years later, my sister is offered the same opportunity and says yes, and I feel hurt as I witness my mom pour her attention and praise onto my sister. I vividly remember sitting in the family room one day, watching yet another movie for my sister's project, while my mom offers her ongoing guidance and support. I express jealousy and anger at all the attention my sister is receiving, and my mom tells me I have no right to feel this way because I had my chance for the same opportunity but said no.

Even after all these years and tons of processing work around this event, I can still feel the sensation of the rug being pulled out from under me as I recall this moment, can still feel my breath stop and my cheeks sting. Despite not getting the support I needed years before to navigate through my fear and say yes to that opportunity, I am being told I'm at fault for allowing my fear to say no. I feel betrayed all around – but especially by my own fear for causing this deeper separation and pain. Fear gets further imprinted in my being, alongside self-blame, betrayal, and shame. And a deep lack of trust in my ability to make the "right" choice takes root.

These moments in time weren't particularly big or traumatic – they'd certainly seem inconsequential to my parents and anyone else – but I know they were significant in forging how I came to relate to fear.

We are born with all of the emotions, yet none of the skills for how to navigate them. We depend on our caregivers to model these skills for us, by acknowledging and labeling our feelings, empathizing with us and normalizing what we feel, and staying with us while we experience them. But these skills for emotional resilience were not often taught to our parents, nor to *their* parents before them.

When the greater culture doesn't value healthy emotional skills or intentionally teach them, the next generation gets handed the same legacy of devaluation, dysfunction, and shame around emotions.

Each one of us does the best we can with what was modeled to us. When we become parents ourselves, we might have every intention of comforting our children when they feel scared and showing them how to work through their fears. But our children's behavior can trigger memories in us. When we see them swept up in anxiety or panic, our bodies remember that fear is threatening. Our nervous systems declare, "Feeling fear leads to rejection, abandonment, or humiliation!" and our primal brains leap into action: "ALERT! DANGER! Shut that feeling down now!"

And despite all our best efforts, we can hear ourselves saying the same sorts of dismissive and invalidating things to our children like, "There's nothing to worry about!" or "You're making a bigger deal about this than you need to!" Or, we may find ourselves shaking our heads in bafflement and walking away.

I have certainly lived this myself. My children frequently experience anxiety, and it's painful looking back on the way I've dealt with it in the past. I always thought I had their best intentions in mind, trying to get them to use reason, encouraging them to push through their fear so they didn't let it conquer them, or trying to distract them from their fear. But I know now that there's a difference between managing fear and invalidating it. Telling people their fear isn't real or warranted doesn't make the feelings they're experiencing miraculously disappear.

Because the feeling of fear is real. Fear always shows up for a reason: something has set off an alarm in our nervous systems and is alerting us to pay attention. We either need to get ourselves to safety immediately ... or sit with our fear, show it compassion, and get curious about what threat it is perceiving, so we can decide what action is truly needed.

These days, when I notice I'm being run by fear – for example, I'm awake in the middle of the night ruminating in anxious thoughts – my new practice is to give myself permission to feel it. I find a quiet space where I can be alone. I come into stillness and breathe deeply. I give my fear a voice by journaling the story it's telling me. But most of all, I connect to that younger part of myself. "Oh, my dear," I tell her. "I feel how anxious you are – there are so many unknowns. It makes sense that you're afraid. I'm right here, no matter what happens."

Then I find I can release the fear and any other emotions tangled up with it, and I feel calmer and more grounded. I gain clarity on whether the threat is real or perceived (i.e., "remembered"). And I can identify what next step is needed.

Learning to be with my own fear has been a big part of my healing, and I am getting better at holding space for it in my kids and others.

**Emotions the author experienced:**

Fear, loneliness, shame, blame, anger, betrayal, rejection, abandonment, compassion, forgiveness, love.

# EMOTIONAL CHECK-IN

What emotions do you feel in response to the idea of learning to be with fear?

What's your earliest memory of feeling fear, and how did the adults in your life respond?

How does fear show up in your life now, and what permission slip could you give yourself to feel it?

# Permission to see your emotions as gifts

**The Gift of Our Emotions**

*by Marna*

When I was growing up, my parents invented a holiday for my sisters and me called Kids' Day. One day each August, while we were busy swimming in the neighborhood pool, they would set up a treasure hunt by carefully unravelling a ball of yarn for each of us, winding the string around chairs, under tables, through bookshelves (and when we were older, through gutters and around trees!), and tying little presents along the strand for us to discover later. We never knew where the string would lead us next – but our curiosity, patience, and persistence were always rewarded with feelings of thrill, awe, and appreciation.

This memory of following the string to discover gifts has offered me a delightfully playful metaphor for engaging with my emotions.

**I've come to think of noticing, allowing, investigating, and honoring my emotions as being on a treasure hunt for lost parts of myself!**

When I create space to identify and fully feel an emotion, moving the excess energy through me in a productive way, what's left behind is the treasure – the emotion's gift for me to investigate and honor.

This is because each of our emotions tells us what we need to feel more connected to ourselves and others. Each emotion shows us how to express more of our unique essence. Each emotion points us to claim more agency in our lives.

For example, an emotion might be signaling a need for rest, or a boundary I need to set and communicate. An emotion might be pointing to something I need to bring into my life to feel fulfilled ... or to something that's mirroring a troubling behavior of mine that I need to face and correct.

I know that when I make space for an emotion and allow it to move through, I'm often rewarded with some sort of new insight about myself.

Sure, it may not always be a comfortable insight – like, "Oh, I see how I keep giving my power away here, oof" – but it does feel like a gift.

It's as if a piece of myself gets clicked back into place. Aha!

And then I'm frequently struck by a deep sense of wonder and appreciation for just how freaking brilliant our emotions are!

Because each emotion is like a thread that we can follow backward or forward in time.

If we go backward in time, we can discover an invitation to heal and reclaim a lost part of ourselves. It brings us back to a moment in time where a choice was made, a coping strategy was used to survive, a story was made up about how we needed to be, a path was forged.

**Allowing ourselves to fully feel each emotion as it arises, we also get an opportunity to nurture ourselves through it in a way we weren't as children.**

If we follow the thread forward, we can discover a gift of insight about what we need and desire in this lifetime.

Imagine, for a moment, we're noticing heat rising in our chest and face. We hear ourselves say: "Well, it's your fault! If you hadn't just..." Ah, we're following the thread of blame!

But oh, where is it leading?... I think there's another feeling underneath. Let's follow it...

Ooh, I recognize it. It's the "It's not fair!" storm of anger...

But there's something else! We may notice some tears stinging our eyes: Hurt is here!

... Oh! And now we have a memory flash from when we were a child and felt emotionally abandoned by our parents in a time of need...

We've arrived at an opportunity for healing, if we feel ready.

Bringing ourselves back to that feeling of deep hurt, of feeling abandoned in a moment when we needed comfort and guidance, we can offer ourselves compassion and reassurance. We can tell ourselves we were right to feel hurt, it wasn't our fault. We can tend to that younger part of ourselves in pain, offer them compassion and love. And we can acknowledge the story we made up about ourselves in that moment ... and then choose to write a new story.

The emotions point us towards where we need healing, where there's a lost part of us waiting to be acknowledged, affirmed, and forgiven.

Emotions are the signs, the flags, the lighthouses, showing us the way toward everything we need to feel whole again. Emotions point the way back home to our whole selves!

And emotions also show us what we need to give ourselves in the future to feel whole.

So, in this way, I invite us to view emotions like clues on a treasure hunt for our wholeness. My wish for you is that you see it's safe to have your emotions, and that you can develop a lighter relationship with them.

**Emotions the author experienced:**

Passion, compassion, awe/wonder, appreciation.

# The Gifts of Emotions
*by Owen*

Recently I stopped in on a dear friend who is dying too young of aggressive cancer.

She is very sick and living. An incredibly excruciating place to be inhabiting, both physically and emotionally. As I sat with her, she shared that she's about to take her family on a bucket list trip out west to experience big sky country. She seemed very tired, in a lot of pain, and not like someone who should be getting on a plane to go out west. She had a plan and was going to see it through.

I listened and continued to let go of judgment or assumptions and was hit by the Eagles song, "Take it to the Limit." A song her mother and my father used to play at parties back in the late 70s. They'd turn the volume up, beer in one hand, cigarette in the other, and sing along at full volume. They took many Friday nights to the limit! My friend was taking her life to the limit and this may be the last time, or not. Who's to say? What I do know is that as I sat with her, I allowed myself to notice the emotions I was experiencing: the deep sadness and fear for her, the grief ever present, and so much love for her. The joy in hearing her voice shift when she spoke of this trip out west and what I imagined was going to be an amazing gift for them all.

Our emotions have many gifts for us, and when we can name them, have an experience of them, and acknowledge their presence and energies, we can stay in the flow. The paradox of emotions is where we truly live. The space of love and fear on the knife edge, a place so real and alive, it's breathtaking.

When I can be with my emotions in the moment and notice their presence and messages, I can listen for the gifts. In my fear, I can feel the love not wanting to be forgotten and the truth felt.

In my anger, I am called to see a boundary has been crossed that needs to be acknowledged, spoken to, and released, so I can feel freedom. In rage, I am brought clarity, energy to make a change, and released to self-authority, well-being, and joy. Lurking in the shadows of the visit with my friend were crisis and overwhelm, which called me to slow down and see what needed to shift. In slowing down, taking a breath, I was able to be with her more fully and notice how deep my sadness and grief were living.

Ah, this is a messy place. A place that inhabits many paradoxical emotions, and we all carry it. This paradox of messiness and gifts, I have learned over the years, is the place where life gets lived and no longer just happens. It takes practice and compassion for all our parts to know that we can recover over and over again as we embrace the mess and gifts of life and death.

It was from slowing down that I could be reminded of our parents and their Friday night fun, "Living life to the limit one more time!" When I left my friend's house and loaded up the Eagles song in my car, I rolled the windows down and let the air blow in as I sang and wept. Releasing the emotions that needed to flow and seeing the gifts. We get this one precious life! How do you want to live it?

So, dear one, as you read this and perhaps notice the experiences in your life that have been in the paradox of emotions, what speaks to you? What do you notice in your unfamiliar senses? How are you living? Have you placed limits on what you can truly feel? I urge you to safely check in with yourself when you notice a pool of paradoxical emotions and see what's present. Have you set limitations on what you can feel? Or perhaps it's a flood that warrants a raft to bring you to shore.

Our emotions have so many messages and gifts as they live together moment to moment.

In honor of my dear friend and sister, I plan on continuing to embrace my emotional landscape and hunt for the gifts, all the while exposing the upper limit of love, joy, hope, and trust.

**Emotions the author experienced:**

Fear, love, joy, self-authority, compassion.

# EMOTIONAL CHECK-IN

What emotions do you feel about viewing your emotions as gifts?

Do any emotions feel more like burdens than gifts, and how do you usually respond to them?

Is there a permission slip you could give yourself that would support you in accepting your emotions as gifts?

# Permission to nurture yourself with compassion

## The Nurturing Voice

*by Owen*

In this book, we write from the place of our nurturing voice. A place we all carry within ourselves. The experience of it is different for each of us, but similar in essence: a place of love, self-love. For me, the voice is one I have come to recognize has been with me since I can remember. She was the early whisper guiding me to love my childhood pets and to receive them as they all decided to use my room as their birthing space. Puppies in my closet and kittens in my drawers.

At the time, I was not conscious of this voice but rather experienced it as a knowing that would roll in. Over time, I have developed this listening and voice and learned to receive her more graciously. She does not shame or blame, there is no drama or martyr pity party – that would be her opposite, the negative ego (who, by the way, can be quite masterful). My nurturing voice comes when I can settle myself, notice my feet planted on the earth, and take a breath.

She shows up in love and grace. There is an embodied experience of a warmth and ease across my chest and heart, softening my belly, I breathe and listen. She can be fierce, firm and rooted in so much love that it can take my breath away. Other times it's a quieter, softer voice that reaches out with a hand to hold mine, or leans in for a hug or a glance of deep love. A knowing, a familiarity and a holding. My heart.

This voice has been developed and nurtured over the years and sits beside my wise adult self.

Aligned in love. I know this sounds a little woo woo, but if you really get quiet and listen to the essence of your nurturing voice, it's embodied – you can taste it, smell it, and sometimes it shows up to be witnessed.

When I am experiencing constricting emotions like fear, terror, rage, blame, etc., I know from years of practice that these emotions must be acknowledged, witnessed, and experienced so that I may hear the nurturing voice in her true essence.

When we have trauma in our lives it can be challenging to trust the nurturing voice. It's often important to hear it from outside ourselves to know we have it in ourselves. This is why community and emotional fitness are so important for well-being. Places we can bring the emotions, be witnessed, and heal.

**What the nurturing voice isn't:**
Small
Niggling
Pitiful
Revengeful
It doesn't shame or blame
There is no back talk or story creating
It does not lead you astray

**The nurturing voice is:**
Often a whisper
A knowing hand on your back
A soft gentle feeling in your heart
The glance of a loved one who knows you, reflecting back the truest truth: love.

A guided knowing
It lands in your body with ease
It's fierce and hot
It will call out in your honor with the depth of truth only your heart
It can hear, or cool and calm
It has a clarity that is solely for you
It's always here for you
Just listen
Trust
It's forgiving and loving
It can be with others' pain and hold yours
Love-filled
Fierce
Kind
Abundant
Possibilities
Quiet
Listens
Warmth
All-knowing
Holds your heart

Emotions the author experienced:

Fear, terror, rage, blame, love.

## Untangling the True Nurturing Voice from Misinformed Beliefs

*by Maggie Pierce*

An invitation ... that's what Owen's words of the nurturing voice are for me. Sharing her experience of how this seemingly external part of her has been known, welcomed, and integrated within her since childhood, opens more of an invitation to me to know my own nurturing voice tucked and hidden away in me.

Examples for me to tap into my nurturing voice get bogged down in the distraction of the voices and perceptions from my real-life parents. While my parents offered me life and a good basis to become a healthy adult, their words could feel like a disconnect that would penetrate harshly, cutting through a sensitive, young child. And since parents are perceived to be the primary nurturer for a child, I collapsed the experience of a critical parent voice into that of a quasi-nurturing parent. By having friends like Owen and other coaching colleagues, I have been offered examples and exposure to witness the healing power of true nurturing voices that warm my heart and have rich influences on my life. Words of encouragement, reassurance, confidence, empowerment, support, belief that I matter, and strength to lean into at times. Our world is sorely missing the comforting words and assurance of a healthy nurturing parent!

The understanding and exposure of the nurturing voice for and with ourselves is so worth the journey of discovery and integration. While we each develop our own maps to this discovery, I hope you, dear reader, will sit with this piece as an invitation to know this nurturing voice as real and true within you. Just imagine hearing the nurturing voice reassuring you in your ear, while negative thoughts/inner words no longer penetrate. Allow these examples to arise within you, and start to hear new soft, energetic words of comfort, reassurance, and more – what a wonderful world this will create!

**Emotions the author experienced:**

Confusion, hurt, betrayal, hope/trust, love.

## Developing a Nurturing Voice

*by Marna*

Until a few years ago, I didn't realize I wasn't particularly nurturing towards myself. I'd always considered myself to be a very nurturing person – but it turns out my nurturing was directed towards others.

A lot of my self-talk consisted of telling myself how to act, what to say, and how to improve. I mistook it to be helpful. I now know that this internal voice was only trying to ensure that I fit in, performed well, met others' expectations, and kept the people around me happy. Yet to do this, it had to dismiss my emotions as incorrect and impractical – they would only get in the way of accomplishing things and getting approval. Decades of dismissing my emotions meant that I consistently ignored what I wanted and needed, and constantly telling myself I could always "be better" meant that I was perpetually unhappy with who I was. So, it turns out, there wasn't anything truly nurturing about the way I related to myself.

In recent years, I have learned what a nurturing presence feels and sounds like, mostly from having space held for me by fellow coaches who witnessed my emotions without judgment, and who normalized and validated what I was feeling.

A nurturing presence feels for me like a gesture that says: *I'm right here.* I can be in the middle of crying, when I suddenly have the urge to put my hand on my heart.

This gesture was first introduced to me by other coaches, who invited me to place my hand on my heart to connect to a younger part of me that was deeply hurt – and in doing so, I took on the role of a nurturing observer. After trying it several times, it felt right to keep doing it. This simple gesture forms an instant line of compassion and comfort for me, and I experience a deep feeling of being seen, heard, and understood.

Making that gesture often creates the safety to feel even more deeply, and my tears increase for a time. But instead of loneliness, there's a warmth in my heart as I feel it all.

When there's a pause between sobs, I can feel spaciousness. And I can hear a voice.

It's validating: *Oh, my dear. It hurts. It makes sense that you're feeling this way.*

It's normalizing: *You're trying so hard. You're human. You made a mistake. You're learning.*

Above all, it's comforting: *I'm right here with you. Take all the time you need.*

Many of us did not hear these messages when we were growing up. As adults, we can sit with those internalized younger parts of ourselves and give them the comfort they have been longing to receive.

**Emotions the author experienced:**

Regret, loneliness, shame, love, compassion, forgiveness.

## The Inner Nurturer is So Much More than a Nurturing Voice
*by Holly*

One of the most healing moments of my life was imagining my younger self being given a hug when she was in a state of despair and hopelessness. It allowed my body to feel safe and nurtured. Today when I feel those emotions, rather than my body being triggered into a state of fear, I imagine receiving the world's most loving hug and it helps the emotion move through me with ease.

The self-nurturer can come to you as a voice, but it also comes in many other forms. Repeating nurturing phrases to ourselves is often helpful. Hearing them from others in real life and from recordings can be even more soothing. Voice is the audio part of your sensory system. You can experience the self-nurturer through all five senses: sound, sight, touch, taste, and smell. Here are some examples of ways in which you might connect with the resource of your self-nurturer:

**Auditory:** The confidence-boosting and compassion-inducing words of another person. The words of a song that stops you in your tracks as someone else has experienced this same thing. The poem that elicits a powerful emotion. A moment of laughter. The morning mantra or affirmation that helps you begin your day. The orchestral music that makes you want to move or feel in a certain way. Singing or screaming out loud, sometimes even swearing or saying the things you've been holding in. The beat of a drum that quiets the inner critic. Birdsong, wind in the trees, or the sound of waves at the beach.

**Visual:** When a person looks at you with that certain gaze, or you imagine this, which lets you know you're not alone. You see their micro-facial expressions. The piece of art that you find so powerful and moving, or uplifting. The object you see in a dream or imagine experiencing on your vision board. A symbol such as the Flower of Life, a mandala, a word. The video in your mind of a certain memory, place, or time. The soothing colors of flowers in spring. The clothes you choose to wear, or make-up you get creative with. The face of a loved one or image of a pet.

**Kinesthetic:** The authentic hug that lets you know you're not alone is using the sense of touch. The pet coming close when they know you're upset. A caring hand placed on your shoulder. Tingles through your body. Nerves twitching. A sense of heat or coldness. A flush of energy moving. A breeze brushing against your skin. Goosebumps. The rise and fall of your chest as you breathe. The feeling of a material or substance on your skin, like soft wool, warm water, sand. The holding of your hand. Writing with a pen and paper. Dancing ecstatically around the house, or anywhere you love. Sports. Throwing things, hitting things in a safe and releasing way, like a cushion, or going to a smash room. (Yes, that's a thing! You, a bat, and things to smash for 30 minutes!)

**Olfactory:** Smells can evoke deep memories, often from childhood or periods of intense feeling. This sense is special because it's the only sense that bypasses the consciousness detector (thalamus) part of the brain. Think pine trees at Christmas, the scent a loved one wears, coffee brewing, bread baking. The essential oils you love, or incense you burn. The earthy ground after rain or dryness after sun. The smell of land after being at sea. The smell of a newborn baby. The smell of a favorite woodland, wax for your surfboard, suncream.

**Gustatory:** Close your eyes and imagine biting into a rich, juicy lemon. Does your mouth water? That's the power of this sensory experience. Certain tastes can make us feel nurtured. It's more than the tongue, though – the whole digestive system can be noticed. If you've ever had a gut feeling, your stomach in knots or rumbling, or found that you get constipated (or the opposite) in certain circumstances, then this might be a strong sense for you. The phrase, "I need some time to digest that" is often used by people who process with this sense. Nurturing gustatory responses have a sense of relaxation, release, expansion, or flow and balance to them.

The entire sensory system helps us to notice incoming stimuli, process them, and choose a response. Our sensory system can signal other things than the nurturing voice. You may be more attuned to one or several sensory systems, and therefore find it easier to connect with and use your self-nurturer through other senses than the voice, audio, or dialogue.

When I was learning about emotions, I struggled with being asked to come up with kind words for myself. I seem to receive information most easily through audio, then process information kinesthetically and output it visually. So, when people said I should scream to release anger, it really didn't work for me.

Sometimes my coaches didn't understand this and responded as if I had a block or resistance. The feedback was that I was doing something wrong, choosing to numb out. What was really going on was that I needed to pound my feet on the ground by going for a run, place my hands in the earth as I gardened to feel grounded, throw a cushion at the wall, or dance till I burned off the excess energy. Doing this with the intention of being with anger or rage, I felt my heart move to more expansive ideas. Movement matters for me as a way of nurturing myself.

My self-nurturer resource often comes to me as the most loving hug I can imagine, and it makes me feel I'm not alone. I've experienced it as the softest white blanket on my skin that cocoons me and keeps me warm. I take baths with nice oils, as the heat and smells instantly relax my physical body. I regularly experience tingles throughout my body or in certain areas as my self-nurturer calls my attention to something, whereas my fellow authors experience it more easily through music, or visual arts, or the words of others.

I do find it useful to experience the self-nurturer in all of the senses, but in the beginning, noticing the sensory form that comes most easily to you for receiving, processing, and outputting information can be helpful. You can consider this throughout this book. Sometimes it works well to switch up the way you nurture yourself by shifting into a different sense.

As the authors share their own stories, you may find certain phrases resonate with you. Highlight them and ask yourself: What sensory system is being used here? Taking a moment to do that will help you recognize what works best for you.

**Emotions the author experienced:**

Frustration, self-authority, passion, well-being.

# EMOTIONAL CHECK-IN

What emotions are you feeling in response to the idea of nurturing yourself?

What do you notice about the way you speak to yourself and the sensory systems you use to nurture yourself?

Is there a permission slip you could give yourself to develop your nurturing voice?

# Permission to love yourself and all your parts

**All Parts of Us Matter!**

*by Marna*

Why does it matter that you, dear reader, experience your emotions?

Because YOU matter.
All parts of you.

Experiencing your emotions lets you reconnect to these parts and reclaim them!

You have parts within that are wise beyond measure and deserve to be heard.
You have parts that you bury way down deep because you're ashamed of them.
There are parts that feel alive, playful, curious, full of wonder, free.
And others that were shattered in a thousand pieces.
You have parts within that are deeply loving.
You also have parts that feel harsh and judging.
There are parts that feel cut off, dismissed, cast away.
And parts that rise up at inconvenient times, bringing pain and suffering.

You have parts within that are fiercely determined to speak up, to take a stand!

And parts that feel powerless.

You have parts that are longing to feel connected to something much greater than yourself.

We all have these parts.

...And they all want so badly to feel heard, loved, and to know they belong!

When we allow our emotions to be true,
It's like we are letting those parts know
"I'm here."
"I'm listening."
"You matter."

When we allow our emotions to be there,
It's like we're giving our parts a voice.
They can tell us what they want,
What they need
To feel whole again.

We ARE whole.
And we deserve to FEEL whole.

**Emotions the author experienced:**

Compassion, self-authority, love, passion.

## My Victim Travels with Me…
*by Owen*

We travel…

I've let you go
over time
no longer sharing
the same suitcase.

Traveling side by side.
Holding hands
one on top of the other,
my younger part
always witnessing me.

Sometimes rolling in
to share her voice
the voice of Worthlessness
Shame, Despair, and Fear.

I feel you here.
We merge
just for a moment –
a trigger,
a reminder
I am only human.

You are the voice of
my Victim,
the one who hurts,
body marked
by events in time –
you are a voice
loud and fierce,

exhausted.

Dear one,
It's time to
lay your head down
and rest.
I have you now.
We are safe,
together
always.

I love you.

Emotions the author experienced:

Worthlessness, shame, despair, fear, love.

## Staying Ashamed Keeps Me Locked in Shame
*by Maggie*

Years of forgetting, numbing, and denial didn't build a strong enough wall to hold back the effects of a raw trauma I was exposed to as a little one. Decades would pass before a deeply hidden truth could be given permission to surface. Time was needed. Perhaps time heals all wounds.

As a child I was (and still am) a huge fan of the movie, *The Wizard of Oz*. I remember its annual presentation on TV, and how I progressed through the years to be able to watch more of the scary parts. In my younger years, the flying monkeys terrified me as they were directed by the Wicked Witch of the West to fly into the sky to find and chase down Dorothy and her innocent little dog, Toto. I can still remember running out of the TV room when that portion of the movie was playing, and even looking up in the sky at night with a fear that those flying monkeys were real enough to be in my neighborhood.

It took years of "eye-covering" or hiding under the blanket to get myself to a point of pushing down the fear to actually watch that part of the movie. My young body was storing that fear-filled emotion, though I didn't have an understanding of it. I learned later that emotions are not logical. I just thought I was becoming brave. Many years of watching the Wizard opened my eyes to the overarching theme of the story, "You've had it all along." That theme metaphorically spoke to the life lessons found when you return to your home after journeying to what seemed like "greener pastures" – a place we often do not recognize for its value until we face challenges that call us home and return us safely to its open door.

The human psyche has layers – sometimes called parts – that develop to protect and love us. These parts within us are ways of survival that are normal, loving, protective, and can be quite reassuring when we get to know them. They can be unknown or seem dormant when our lives are in alignment. This is very normal. Also normal is the integration of parts that can develop and become exposed when life gets shaken up a bit (chaos).

Our parts are developed to protect us at times when we need them most, and that's most likely when we are very young. Even with the best of parents and surroundings, a little one can need additional layers of love and protection to feel safe to move through life and life experiences.

In my childhood experience of watching *The Wizard of Oz* in a safe environment, cuddled up with caring parents, I was still feeling a need for another layer of protection and love, except I didn't know how to ask for that. We are now beginning to recognize how trauma can occur on a smaller, though still very impactful level to a developing psyche. These traumatic experiences can have a continuous impact (emotionally, mentally, and physically) on our lives, even if we try to push them into a "closet" to hide the pain.

Years later, in my 50s, I was attending an intensive Voice Dialogue workshop for my coaching profession. I was staying in a room with a colleague when I suddenly woke up in the middle of the night from a nightmare. As I settled myself down to tell her about it, I saw myself as Dorothy in *The Wizard of*

Oz, when the Wicked Witch rides on her broomstick to write in dark letters in the sky, "Surrender Dorothy."

The message being unveiled to me in the same broomstick manner did not come through completely while I was still in the dream-state trance. As I sat quietly, more letters appeared in the sequence that had started in my dream: M-O-L-E-S-T. Suddenly, the forgotten memories that were too scary for a 6-year-old to comprehend were becoming conscious for me to process, out of the lockdown of shame a little one held about herself.

The terminology changed to "rape" from the time this 6-year-old faced the terror of being molested, but the shame was still there. The experience of that day flashed back in full detail – the colors, the smells, the lighting all returned in a flash, as if the memories had been frozen in time waiting for my visit.

I felt as if I was still that young girl – confused, trying to run away, and so very afraid of so many things – all of it flashed through my memories. I could feel my little one's body running up a hill as fast as she could to get away, as if those monkeys were chasing her, until she got into the house and ran to her bedroom. She closed herself in the closet and sat on the wood floor for hours, alone and scared. In the darkness of the closet, she tried to calm this terrifying hurt that she had no reference point for understanding. This little one felt shame and assumed it was her fault. She shut down a part of her at that time and did not tell anyone, because she thought she would be blamed and get in trouble. She stuffed it all down and swallowed her pain and confusion. She never told anyone for years, while the shame kept piling up within her and influencing her life choices in consistent, subtle ways.

This is how a part that has been emotionally traumatized becomes isolated energetically within a functioning human life. Most of us have this within us in one form or another, often without our awareness.

I did not feel fully safe from that day forward, because that part of me was influencing me like a filter on a lens. I felt like I always had to watch my back. I had numerous panic attacks soon after that day that my parents never understood; to them, it was as though the attacks were occurring out of the blue. I was too young to understand what my body was trying to tell me. The denial was taking hold. I did not know how to ask for comfort or lean in for support, mostly because I was still feeling ashamed and thinking I was bad. I built an emotional wall where I would depend on myself to work things out for a lifetime.

As I would see later, the misconstrued and misdirected thoughts and emotions and denial that started immediately after this traumatic event were my psyche's way of loving and protecting me, no matter what. My parts were offering the best protection for me, at the maturity level of a 6-year-old, to deal with shame-filled trauma. As I matured into a woman, aspects of shame around this wound kept me from facing what had truly happened. I felt like I had a burning ember of rage that could show up totally out of context.

I sought therapy through EMDR (Eye Movement Desensitization and Reprocessing). I built more support for myself and all my parts as I was able to reveal missing pieces of my childhood – even the parts that had falsely judged and criticized me. I began to realize and let go of the layers I had unknowingly made myself swallow in shame – good girl syndrome, being nice, issues around trust, spiritual obligation, and other personal and cultural stigmas. I felt some relief from the imaginary fingers that I perceived pointing at me, saying that I was at fault and unlovable.

I realized my abandoned little girl needed me to accept her just where she was – to hear how frightened and confused she was. I was being called to listen deeply to my own sadness. I was the one she had been waiting for: the one she could tell what had happened to her, the one who could tell her she didn't need to face this alone. She wanted to be free of the weight of shame. And I realized that I, as an adult, needed to respond to and for her so we could face this trauma together.

The process is still unfolding over many years, and many re-encountered aspects continue to show up. That's the hidden face of shame.

This, dear reader, is my experience. I have not allowed myself to reveal or share it to many because I held the belief that this occurrence and I were still shameful and needed to stay silent. Shame is rooted in the belief that I AM BAD – the essence that permeates through and through.

I continue to heal this deep wound within myself through dedication to self-acceptance, and in doing so I offer that healing for others before and after me. I am giving myself permission to give back the shame to the wounded person that my six-year-old encountered. He gets to own and hold the shame and responsibility for his behavior, not me.

I hope that anyone reading my story that relates in any way to these circumstances (and I know there are many) will face this inner shame with the courage it takes and give it back to its rightful owner. Our silence needs to take on a voice.

It is not your fault. It is not your fault. It is not your fault.

You are safe.
You are held.
It is not now, and never was, your fault.
I love you ... All parts of you.

## Emotions the author experienced:

Fear, anxiety, guilt, sadness, confusion, resentment, freedom.

# Celebrating Yourself: Feeling Your Way from Victim to Vitality

*by Holly*

Following Maggie's brave piece, acknowledging a great collective wound that keeps on being shamed and pushed into the shadows, I feel it's important to say, "Me too." Maggie inspires me to join what feels to me like a healthy rebellion to pull back our power. One where people of all genders and identities are uncovering this all-too-common wounding and saying we're going to love ourselves enough to be with the parts of us exiled to the darkness.

Between the ages of 5 and 7, I was sexually abused. Like Maggie, I only remembered it when I finally left home for university and found a sense of safety. I wrote in my diary back then, "Are these memories even real? Am I going crazy? How would anyone believe me if I don't even believe myself?" I felt confused, doubtful, shamed, and guilty. I didn't have the emotional range back then to admit I was outraged, resentful, feeling violence towards the perpetrator and especially the people who failed to protect and support me.

We share these stories, knowing you could feel uncomfortable reading or hearing them. You're allowed to feel uncomfortable and anything else. Perhaps your first response was sadness, compassion, love, or even shame for your own experiences too? It has taken me a long time to be comfortable talking about this topic, and I still have to remind myself that it's okay to do that.

Everyone experiences events of wounding or neglect; it's sort of a universal process. I ask that as an individual you move towards the emotions you feel in response to these stories, rather than away from them. When more of us can acknowledge such events and the many different wounds that are held in the shadows, the healing can begin. A shift in culture is initiated.

I have a habit of journaling to process my emotions, especially the more constricting and heavy ones. This week, I noticed that I rarely journal on the light and expansive emotions. (Constricting emotions being those that take me down, and expansive being those that uplift me.) I have to admit that the idea of writing to celebrate myself brings up a lot of inner dialogue. Somehow it feels big-headed and improper. But another habit is to move towards the resistance, as there is always juicy stuff there. So, let's give this a whirl.

Deep down, I am trying to create a story and identity I am proud of, instead of one that leaves me entangled in shame and powerlessness. I want to give myself permission to live with a certain kind of joy and vitality rather than victimhood. I want to ensure I don't get trapped in helplessness, where I burn up my energy trying to prove that I'm good, not bad; lovable, not shameful; worthy, not abandoned; can belong and not be rejected.

When you tell a story of your struggles and wounds, past or present, an important question to explore is, "Why are you telling it?"

I've found there are three reasons I tell stories:

> To leave or let go of something.
>
> To change something.
>
> To accept something.

Often that something is our emotions. The motivation behind telling your stories may be to change how you feel, let go of feelings that are constricting you, or accept how you really feel. Emotions can control your thoughts. Humans are also massive meaning-makers, where stories also carry beliefs about the experiences you describe. These thoughts can equally affect your feelings. There is a dynamic system at play where mind, emotion, and body can affect each other in any direction.

My deepest longing is to experience more joy, more passion, and more vitality. I'm exploring how to create that reality for myself. Isn't it interesting that there is a tendency to overly focus on the pain and struggles, and how naturally that comes and flows through us? Yet something inside tells me that feeling okay, celebrating who I am, is somehow a bad thing – to the extent that it feels unnatural.

### Reflections on letting go

My sense is that being able to write about expansive emotions could shift my perspective on my life story. If I claim this uplifting version of my story, then my ego and the masks I wear have to drop away. It feels like I'm dying in a way. I let go of the strong version of me and invite in the vulnerable and sensitive parts. I let go of the pain, and perhaps find a gift.

There is a certain amount of courage required for me to go here, to let go of the old, wounded identity and identify with a deeper and more intrinsic essence of myself. My authentic self. This empowered version of my story is what I want to experience more of. A story that transmutes the fate I was born to, into my chosen destiny. Daring to live the life I want for myself, with great love for all that has shaped me.

### Reflections on changing my thoughts and feelings

One of the barriers to this is the ideas and beliefs I carry. I was told that being resentful made me a bad person – that if I resented my abuser and the adults who let me down, it would trap me in pain and suffering. I have frequently been instructed by well-meaning professionals, friends, and close ones to find forgiveness. Justifications have been suggested such as wounded people "know not what they do" and "honor thy mother and father." As a result, I didn't let myself feel the intensity of emotions brewed up inside me, in case I ended up in hell.

When keeping my emotions suppressed inside became a living hell, it was enough to make me question the beliefs and advice. I needed to acknowledge that my feelings of rage, violence, and despair were normal and necessary, given what I experienced. The purpose of these emotions was to help me make a change. To restore my personal boundaries, to find my voice in saying "No" to what I don't want to experience, to express my needs, and to claim my power to create my reality, despite the very real truth of being a victim.

### Reflections on acceptance

I have found the greatest sense of inner peace by simply giving myself permission to feel the most constricting emotions. The sooner my feet touch the bottom, the sooner I can push off and head back up to the surface for fresh air and sunshine.

It is only in feeling my feelings fully that I can experience this lighter, more energized space of being. I am feeling my way from victim, beyond victory, and into vitality.

My victim or wounding story holds all the bad things that happened to me: the abuse, the neglect, the disconnection, the lack of safety, the trauma of unprocessed emotions. I have not always accepted these events as they happened. I held the resonance of wanting reality, life, to have happened in a different way than it did. I was in a state of rejecting life. I was telling life, and the events and people, YOU SHOULD NOT HAVE HAPPENED TO ME THIS WAY!

It is a losing game, trying to change what cannot be changed.

Whatever happened to you happened.

I do not mean to be dismissive of how you feel or to minimize the impact of your own wounding events. No, I encourage you to be with the full extent of your feelings about those experiences. Those feelings are 100% valid. What I am saying is that when you accept that this is what happened, it is a matter of fact, it opens the door to a new possibility. You can see the pain, hold it in loving compassion, and see yourself and your life as already whole, enough, divine. You can see through the illusion of brokenness and accept that you have the power to decide how what happened in the past will shape your life from this point forward.

There is a peculiar thing that happens when we tell our stories from a healing energy. Others who don't have that emotional range yet may feel uncomfortable and project their discomfort towards you, as if you and your story are making them uncomfortable. It's easy to doubt yourself and wonder what you did wrong. The reality is they may be feeling their own discomfort and blaming you for it. It's important to remember that how others perceive you is not a reflection of who you are; it's a reflection of their own inner world – the lens they look through.

For me, acceptance is when I can share who I am and my story, if I choose to or not, and feel okay no matter how someone else responds. Acceptance is when I am grounded in love, self-authority, and compassion for myself and others. My victim stories hold me in a false reality, dreaming of the ideal fairy tale of how life should have been so that I did not have to experience this. My self-nurturer says, *Oh, but you did experience it, and if you let yourself feel what you feel, then you do not have to keep on re-experiencing that pain. Feeling your emotions can restore your sense of unity.*

At the heart of a victim story is pain, and the avoidance of that pain keeps you feeling it more intensely than is necessary and repeating that same experience over and over. There are many ineffective ways of trying to get to that sense of deep acceptance. I have travelled down many a cul-de-sac myself – into the feelings of overwhelm, blame, anger, confusion, frustration, doubt, worry, guilt – and I can tell you this: these strategies may give us short-lived relief, but they are not the real solution.

These are dead ends where we can't find a way out, no matter how hard we try. We don't get to experience what we truly long to experience. This is known as an overcoming story. Our feelings help us know what we want, and only by feeling can we understand and know this. It is a step forward from the victim story. Then the question becomes, "How do I break through to my great life story?" By noticing and celebrating who I am.

### Celebrating myself

I am a brave soul who has known the depths of despair and the highs of choosing to listen to my heart and soul. I made a choice to find myself and lost my family in the process. The devastation has been raw and tender, and the gifts abundant. I would not wish my life to have been another way. It allows me this phenomenal insight into the workings of our inner world, and the interconnectedness of our outer world. I have created a better life for myself, though the value of that is more visible on the inside than outside of my life. I am rediscovering my creative, passionate, expressive parts, and I delight in them. I am a paradox of seriousness and playfulness, intelligence and daftness, love and hate. I love all that I feel, and all the parts of me who feel them.

# EMOTIONAL CHECK-IN

What emotions do you feel around loving yourself and all your parts?

What parts are you aware of in yourself, and can you offer a name for these characters within you?

    I have a part that....

    I have a part that...

    I have a part that...

Is there a permission slip that would support you in loving any part of yourself more?

# Permission to know that you're enough

**Dare to Live**

*by Holly*

Know this dear reader...
Your being born makes you worthy.
You are innately loveable.
The illusion is that you think there is something wrong with you,
that it was your fault.

It was not your fault.
You were just the little one.
It was too much for you.
Too much was expected of you.
Wounded adults couldn't see past their own pain.
Wounded adults couldn't hold space for your emotions.
They feared their own feelings.

Out of love, you have carried so much for others.
This is a sign.
Your sign

to transform the guilt and shame.
You do that by letting yourself feel.
Own your experiences and truths,
they are yours.

Your feelings and experiences are allowed to be different to how others feel.
You have a right to feel how you felt in those moments.
You are allowed to feel that way.
There are no good or bad emotions.
Emotions are like messengers of wisdom,
They whisper how to heal.

If you can notice them,
Say thank you to them.
Thank and thank and thank again.
Notice how your senses change as you say thank you.

Realize the truth:
You are enough.
You are loved.
You are deserving.
You are valued.
You are love.

Emotion is energy.
Energy cannot be destroyed, only transformed.
Transform it by feeling.
Restore flow.
Reduce resistance by updating the meanings,
update the beliefs you make from your stories.

Be you.

Be unashamedly you.
Be at peace.
Be.
Give yourself permission to be.

Let your being fly.
Let your voice shine.
Let yourself be seen.
Let it all be felt.
Don't let it go.

Let it in.
Let it be.
Be with it.

Feeling is living.
To feel deeply is to fully live.
Dare to live.

**Emotions the author experienced:**

Love, self-authority, passion, wellbeing.

## My Journey with the Mother Wound
*by Holly*

It's one thing to be encouraged to feel your feelings. It's another thing to know how to do that and trust you'll be safe. The following piece is me giving myself permission to say and feel what I do about my relationship with my mother. It describes the tangle with my wounds; what I needed and longed to experience as a child and adult, but didn't; and how I eventually figured out how to nurture myself, with the help of a mentor. Many different parts of myself are speaking. This is the brilliant chaos that's sometimes inside of me.

I can't say that this is written about one particular event; it's a muddle of things. It's the messy feelings arising in me from being a six-year-old unable to tell my mother I was being abused because she put too many of her own worries on me as a child. I knew at that age that my mother was terrified of social services taking my sister and me away from her. That she could take her own life if I did speak of it, and definitely would if the police were involved.

Twenty years after this, I decided to change my career path away from engineering and into the world of training and coaching. My mother told me I was crazy for making this choice, and she cut me off. We were estranged for many years, with no contact. It hurt like hell, yet I numbed it out. I made up a story that perhaps she thought it would make me change my behavior and stay an engineer.

I also thought that my mother wanted to be able to boast about what a great job she'd done of producing this successful offspring, despite her own victim story – that my being an engineer gave her a story about her own self-worth. She was very proud of me, and of herself for helping me become an engineer against all the odds of our background. I was proud, too, and I'm grateful for what she was able to give me. It was enough to set me free from a life of poverty and powerlessness. I know my life is all the better for how she shaped me towards education and loved me in the best way she knew.

My soul was burning bright, though, calling me to live the way I needed to, to expand into who I am and explore the world more fully. To explore my potential beyond the confines of survival-based living. I recognized my privilege in having this choice that my mother never had the luxury of making. Yet I felt like I was living a half-life, trying to please everyone but myself. I believed I had more to offer the world, and I had promised myself at six years old that I would get through to being a grown up, instead of taking my one life, and do something good with all that happened to me.

Destiny was calling me. Having the courage to step out of a safe, secure job and follow my passion is one of the things I am most proud of in my life. Especially as it has also brought me so much joy. For many years, I wished it could have been different between my mother and me. Some years later we reconnected for a while, before her criticisms and threats of estrangement in attempts to control me became too much.

I walked away from the relationship because my mother was too busy finding faults in me, while I was overlooking hers. I needed to feel okay about myself, that I had some intrinsic value and worth. I needed space to heal myself. I struggled with guilt and shame for a very long time while I avoided my emotions. My mother made sure I knew she sacrificed to get me where I am, yet she didn't acknowledge my own sacrifices or that there could even have been any. This was love with very large strings attached. The payment due: one soul.

My fear has always been that people will think I'm a bad person for having these feelings and making the choices I've made. What matters most, though, is that I stop abandoning myself and love myself enough to say I am allowed to have boundaries.

It's easy to imagine that emotional abuse is not as bad as physical abuse, yet they light up all the same areas of the brain. Both types of abuse hurt us in very real ways. I tried speaking to my mother about this for a lifetime, until I accepted that she was always going to hurt me, as she believed her actions were loving. My job was to stop abandoning myself and let go of trying to please her. That was my breakthrough, my release from my self-made cage.

I chose to protect myself from unhealthy behavior by remaining estranged after the last time she cut me off. My life is more pleasant, joyful, and abundant without my mother in it, and that is the gift I am giving myself for now. This is discernment, which is very different from judgment. It has a peaceful quality inside my soul. I even found my father and reconnected after having not been allowed to see him and being told many lies.

But that's a story for another time.

## Learning to Let My Light and Shadows Shine

Mother, do you love me? My heart longs to feel that I'm loved just for the essence of my being. Not because I was being who you wanted me to be. Not for what I do or achieve that makes you feel proud or meets some expectation. But just because I exist. Because **I AM.**

I have tried, so very hard, for decades, to be worthy of your love.

I thought that if I could only love you enough and be good enough, then I could earn my place in our family constellation. That I would belong somewhere, be valued and loved. So I obsessively set about making a valuable contribution, being the best, pleasing you and aiming to never make a mistake.

Your love never came.

I struggled to prove to you that I was good enough, and that I deserved your love. No matter how hard I tried, your love never came. I felt broken. Why did this happen to me? What was wrong with me? Why does everyone who's supposed to love me leave me?

As a child, my mind raced to find answers. It must be my fault. I must have been really bad in a past life. If it's my fault, then what do I need to believe to make Mum right?

I am, at my core, bad.
I am to blame if Mum is upset.
I am hurting people.
I am selfish.
I am responsible for keeping everyone safe.
I am of no value.
I am not to make ripples.
I am wrong.

I am resentful.
I am lazy.
I am always to blame.
I am not allowed to have needs.
I am not allowed to matter.

My heart filled with anguish as I gradually turned on myself. My inner critic stepped up to keep me in check.

The gift in this was that I became highly competent at manifesting my desires in many areas of life. I was highly attuned to emotions, as I had tried to intuit yours so that I might gain that sustaining elixir of life called Mum's love.

It was never my fault you treated me as not enough. I never needed to prove my goodness. It was never my role to fill that hole in your soul. **I AM ENOUGH.**

As the hope of connection and wholeness faded, sliding into its place came guilt and shame, followed by pity and anger.

Permission to speak, Little One:

I am so bored by my own stories. Sometimes it feels like I've been looking back in the past, healing, for most of my life. I want to look forward to the future, through the present. I am ready to create, to manifest, to live and love. In a big way. No more hiding in the darkness. I am also lightness.

I'm craving lightness. Fun. Joy. Pleasure. My mentor passed away earlier this month. His energy was vibrant at 76 years young. We were speaking one moment, then he was gone a day later. My heart aches. I miss him. I felt love. He said that to feel is to live and to feel deeply is to live deeply and fully. He gave me an experience of something indescribable, something I'd longed for from my mother.

My mother. What a head case! I'm spinning between stories. I want to scream out loud, "Just fucking look at me." In my mind's eye, I see her turn away in shame and disappointment with me. Guilting me for not being and doing as she expected, demands, and insists. A huge hand appears from the clouds with a pointed finger directed to me. A booming, God-like voice says, "YOU ARE BAD!"

I want to tell the world all of my stories – like a child in the playground seeking backup from friends so that they might help make my voice louder. It's as if I've been screaming at my mother from the depths of my stomach for thirty-six years: "LOOK AT ME, I'M HERE, AND I'M NOT A BAD PERSON."

The experience with my mentor was presence and complete acceptance. It's rare to know you can show up in any state and not have to put on a show or a mask of happiness. Whatever was in me was allowed. All parts were welcome. All feelings were welcome. Whatever was there in my experience was encouraged, without judgment. "Acceptance is the absence of judgment," he'd say.

I don't want him to go. Now I'm without again. I smile as his mischievous presence comes into my mind's eye and reminds me: I have access to all the resources I need. It's not dependent upon him. I feel his presence fading. I'm not worried. There is a sense of an opening. A calling for me to step into being, into my expression, my voice, and to be seen.

But what about my mother? How do I escape this tangled, sticky web of hers that I'm perpetually stuck in? I see my leg pulled free, only to get stuck to the next branch for having feelings. Then the same with my arm. My energy is consumed in this battle to free myself. It's slow progress that'll take longer than a lifetime. I imagine pouring a magical fluid that dissolves the web. Web of emotions, BE GONE!

The look of the death mother is lifted — you know, the look that could turn you to stone. The one that others don't see but has paralyzed you your whole life. Like the female spider, my mother is sucking the blood from her prey. I am drained. There is no blood left to give. I am sucked dry. I give up the struggle. She angers, then decides to walk away, leaving me to die. Alone. Lost. Empty. Only a shell of me there.

No heart. She had no heart. That's why this happened. It wasn't me being bad. She was trying to nourish herself. I was her food. Gnawed at perpetually, for not being able to fill that hole in her soul. The hole where love was supposed to be. She couldn't give me what she didn't have to give. I suffered it and I survived it. I freed myself from the web of entanglements. And my mentor, Dick, helped replenish my shell. He showed me love just for being.

Am I enough? Am I loveable?

I am. I am now.

And yet I still think to myself, oh, how wonderful it would be to have my mother look at me with eyes full of love. Instead, I look at myself with loving eyes and a loving heart. The kind of eyes that Deborah has for her daughter.

### Emotions the author experienced:

Hurt, betrayal, abandonment, rejection, guilt, shame, anger, blame, pity, self-authority, hope, worthlessness, emptiness, compassion, happiness, well-being, love, freedom, healing.

# EMOTIONAL CHECK-IN

What emotions do you feel in response to the idea that you're enough?

Do you ever struggle to believe that you are enough, and in what areas of your life?

Is there a permission slip you could give any part of yourself to know that you are enough?

# *Permission to fall apart*

## Shattering: My Journey through Grief

*by Deborah*

Imagine for a moment that the person you love most in the world has been taken in an instant, as my daughter, Scout, was in a tragic accident in 2019. My heart shattered into a million pieces, like the windshield of her car, shards flying everywhere. I plummeted into a black hole of shock, panic, and total despair. *This can't be true! How can I fix it? How can I breathe? How can I live? How can I escape this bottomless pit?*

Fasten your seatbelt and prepare yourself for a ride that will take you to the edges of what you imagined you could possibly feel – and perhaps beyond – and then return you to the heart of who you truly are (and always have been). A swirling kaleidoscope of emotions, all of them part of you.

---

Sitting in my peaceful sunroom, I reach for my *Work Your Light* oracle deck to glean some inspiration to jumpstart my writing. I shuffle the cards, take a deep breath, and draw one: Initiation. A rite of passage, crossing a threshold. The interpretation says:

> *We are being called to face what scares us and have to be willing to lose it all, in order to gain a new way of being... It is through the seeming hardship that our heart cracks open and our spirit is invited forward... Soon you will bless the thing that broke you down and cracked you open, because the world needs you open...You are being tested because you are headed somewhere sacred. It will be worth it. And you're closer than you think.*

A stunning message. Broken down and cracked open? Hell yes, and then some.

The message that the world needs me open echoes a recent Akashic reading, which told me in no uncertain terms that the community I had cultivated over many years was waiting to hear from me.

Am I willing to face what scares me in order to gain a new way of being? I'm not wild about the idea, but I'm willing to try – especially if the path leads to a sacred place. I know I can call on my Higher Self to help me navigate.

What scares me about sharing this story? Plenty.

I'm afraid that I won't get it right. My Higher Self says: *It's your journey, your truth. You can't get it wrong.*

I'm afraid that if I revisit the emotions of that devastating time, I won't find my way back. I don't want to relive the worst moments of my life. My grieving heart says: *Don't make me do it! It's too hard. It's too painful. I've finally found some equilibrium and can sleep through the night. Why do I have to pick at these scabs?* My Higher Self says: *Because the world needs you open. Because your community is waiting to hear from you. Because you're headed somewhere sacred. You won't get lost. You are always held, and you are never alone.*

I'm afraid that I don't know how to capture it all, where to start, how to untangle this jumble of memories and emotions. My Higher Self says: *Start anywhere. Work from the middle out, or from the end to the beginning, or anywhere in between. It's your story. You can't get it wrong.*

Starting now – in this place, this moment, surrounded by golden light, a sleeping dog nearby. Light years away from the traumatic events that launched my journey through and beyond the depths of grief.

I sit here alone, yet in community with my "sisters-in-writing," each of us crossing a threshold to share how we have been cracked open to find a new way of being. Their courage and commitment fuel my own and help me face my fear. It's time to take the first steps and begin to share my story.

---

This is a story of death and rebirth. Of a journey from drowning in utter despair to reclaiming the possibility of hope and joy. Of finding the courage to shake off conventional notions of what's "proper" and to listen to my heart, even (or especially) when it's leading me into uncharted territory – places I never expected to go, choices I never imagined would be necessary.

If you had shown me the itinerary for this journey, I would have said, "Hell, no! You can't make me go there!" And yet, when I found myself in that unthinkable place, I said, "Hell, no!" to convention and propriety and "Hell, yes!" to the whispers of my heart and soul.

My ears ring and blood pulses through my head as I write this. Just thinking about that time brings back that overwhelming sensation of being forced to make critical decisions when my brain was struggling to comprehend why those decisions were necessary. I felt backed into a corner, gut-punched by emotions left and right: despair, confusion, emptiness, anger, abandonment, fear. "Get me out of here!" I screamed, to no one and everyone. "This can't be happening! I can't fucking do this! Make it stop!"

I'm struck by the irony of writing about this emotional journey as if I've come out on the other side and am now basking in the relief and satisfaction of having made it through alive, if not unscathed. As Scout wrote in one of her teenage journals, "Who am I kidding?"

The truth is, I did come out on the other side of the vortex AND it's not over. Time isn't linear, and neither is grief. Certain triggers or my own train of thoughts can plunge me right back into the maelstrom, including this very moment. Here we go again...

Navigating the vortex hasn't been linear, either. It's like trying to paddle down a river with rapids that could smash you to pieces, eddies that could swirl you around forever, and occasional stretches of calm, glassy water where you can relax and breathe before the next round begins.

I hear a whisper from spirits beyond myself: *We have so much love and compassion for you, dear woman. You were thrown into that turbulence without a moment's notice and found a way to navigate a strange new reality in the midst of your anguish, without trying to change or control it. You held fast to what would keep you on course: deep, abiding love for your girl and a fierce commitment to honor her spirit, no matter what. Painful, beautiful work. Well done.*

---

The Buddha taught us that impermanence is the nature of reality. Nothing stays the same, no matter how desperately we wish it would. We are destined to lose everything we love.

Nothing stays the same, including emotions. As I started to write this passage, the full spectrum of grief showed up and consumed me. I collapsed into myself, convulsing with sobs, tears and snot running down my face. In that moment, boundless grief was the only reality I knew.

Resistance was futile. Nothing to do but surrender, surrender, surrender, again and again ... until the energy dissipated, and calm returned.

The loss endures. Grief wells up, passes through, and moves on. Until the next time...

My journey through grief is teaching me to listen to the whispers of my heart and notice what, or who, shows up. It's a lesson in relinquishing control and receiving what wants to emerge.

I've discovered that the process has three parts: Listen. Trust. Feel.

*Listen* to the whispers. *Trust* what you hear. *Feel* the emotions that arise.

Here's how it showed up one day:

Months after Scout died, I sat at my desk, forehead in palm, cradling a skull that was surprisingly devoid of thoughts at the very moment I had set aside for writing.

I checked in with my heart. More radio static. Ditto with my gut.

Was this serenity, or stubbornness? Indifference, or resistance? In that moment I had no idea.

My surly, frustrated Adolescent chimed in: *I can't do this! Let's shut things down and go home.* (But honey, we are home…)

My little dog was curled up in his bed, not a care in the world. "Maybe he's got the right idea," I thought. "Just crawl into bed, wrap yourself in a cuddly blanket, and be comforted … and alone, again…"

Those last words reverberated in my head. "Alone, again … alone, again … alone…"

Now the feelings tiptoed in. That special blend of sadness, emptiness, love with nowhere to go. Soft tears this time, no heaving sobs (at least, not yet).

A muted despair; an all-too-familiar emptiness that had set up camp and made itself at home.

I remembered the process. *Listen.*

I asked the Emptiness what it needed from me. *Permission. Permission to be recognized and accepted for what I am. Permission to take up space, even if it's just a pallet in a corner of your heart.*

*Welcome me*, said the Emptiness. *Love me. That deep longing to be held is me speaking. Stop trying to fill me up – I need you to trust me and feel me.*

*She's gone, and she's never coming back. You can't change that. Don't try to replace her – it's not possible. Just hold onto your deep love for her. That love will never leave you. Your love is the portal, the through-line, and the lifeline.*

*Trust.* The message stirred up a flurry of emotions. It was time to trust the process and feel them all, knowing I would come out safely on the other side.

*Feel.* Grief and emptiness and love and despair welled up and cracked me open. Tears flowed and splashed on the words I had just written. I put down the pen, wrapped my arms around myself, and took refuge in the familiar comfort of my sofa.

Writing would have to wait. It was time to feel.

---

How do you re-assemble a shattered heart?

I claw my way through life, day by day, seeking scattered shards of my heart in a desperate attempt to make it whole again. I find some in the haunted eyes of those whose hearts were also shattered by the loss of Scout. Some are in the beauty of a sunset, a towering redwood, a cardinal flitting across the yard. Some are in raucous laughter, some in making music, some in sharing stories and memories from years ago and just the other day.

Some shards are clean and shiny, some caked in mud. Some appear in clusters; others remain hidden, perhaps never to be found.

Each recovered shard brings recognition and relief. I put the pieces together little by little, doing the best I can. My reassembled heart is a semblance of what it was before everything fell apart. Recognizable, but never the same. Slightly misshapen, with messy seams. A few missing pieces now exist only in memory, their form and beauty implied by their absence – a fitting reminder of Scout's palpable presence in the hearts of all who loved her, despite her absence from the physical realm.

Messy seams give my reconstructed heart more room for love. It's different now – and larger. Missing pieces create openings for love and light to flow in and out, nourishing myself and the world.

A soft whisper from spirit guides, or perhaps my own heart:

> When the shattering happened, dear one, you tumbled into a deep well of grief and despair. Yet the more you fell apart, the more you cleared a path for healing. Yes, you were out of your mind, but you weren't crazy. Somewhere, somehow, you knew you had to feel before you could heal.
>
> You fell apart over and over and over. You wept and howled like a banshee, thrashed like a furious toddler, spat at the world like an indignant adolescent. "This isn't happening! I can't fucking do this! Get me out of here!"
>
> It happened again and again and again. Yet each time you tumbled into the well, the terrain became a little more familiar – not comfortable, but somehow known and trusted. Less like a dark hole, and more like a portal to somewhere new.
>
> Little by little, you begin to remember who you are and re-member your heart. Each time you emerge from the depths, you open your eyes a little more and see your shattered heart reflected in the eyes of those whose hearts were also broken. You recognize shards of your heart embedded in theirs, and fragments of their hearts in yours. You are not alone.
>
> "I see you," say their ravaged eyes. "I am here," you reply through your tears. Cradling your broken hearts, you stumble forward together, finding solace in loss, easing pain through love.

Re-membering by remembering, healing by feeling. One heartfelt breath at a time ...

Emotions the author experienced:

Despair, emptiness, abandonment, fear, anger, sadness, overwhelm, confusion, love, compassion, hope, trust.

## My Shattered Heart

*by Owen*

My heart is shattered;
Reassembled, then shattered again.
The shattering and reassembling
have come over time with the experiences of
trauma, crisis, overwhelm, loss, and death.

My shattered heart
Has a voice loud and clear,
Bold and vibrant,
Soft and supple,
Sacred and divine.

My shattered heart
Continues to beat
To its own rhythm,
Keeping time
and me, going.
My shattered heart
Bleeds and aches.
Together we
Move through
And find each other again.

My shattered heart
Has memories,
Cellular,
Visceral,
And known.

My shattered heart
Has a map
Of the bonds that tie
and at times
Come undone.

My shattered heart
Knows how to heal,
Even when
I don't
Have a clue.

My shattered heart
Is once again whole,
The torn spaces
Mended with threads
And love.

My shattered heart
Is mine alone,
An intimacy
Of seen
And unseen.
My shattered heart
Comes with me
Always.
"Listen," she says,
Whispering.
We have been shattered

And we have healed.
Don't lose hope,
For tomorrow
Is another day.

**Emotions the author experienced:**

Overwhelm, hope.

# EMOTIONAL CHECK-IN

What emotions do you feel about letting yourself fall apart?

What situations or relationships have shattered your heart?

Is there a permission slip you could give yourself in relation to falling apart?

# *Permission to be vulnerable*

## No Amount of Concealer Can Hide You from the World
*by Maggie*

Don't go in too deep. Skim the surface where it's safe and easy to tread. Skin deep…

I have been a trained licensed aesthetician for over 20 years. I have loads of training in the organ of the skin, the allure of beauty, the significance of health from the inside out, and how much dedication it takes to attend to oneself. Just like the skin, our lives have layers to uncover and attend. My clients would come in regularly for their facials, to address what they were seeing on the surface – the wrinkles, the breakouts, the dryness or the oiliness, the techniques for ageless beauty. Their concerns were mostly about inconvenience: "Do something to get rid of them! I don't want to see this!" Addressing their concerns, I always had the watchful eye and the inquisitive curiosity about what was going on at a deeper level – and there was always another level.

Lying flat on a spa bed and into my healing hands melted away the walls they had worked so hard to build for the world. Softening into vulnerability allowed my clients to expose the dialogue of the emotions deep within. My clients did such an amazing job to hide, to mask, to shield from the outside world. Through this portal, we could journey together. Some clients would want to stay on the surface – the dialogue would stay professional and focused on their concerns. I always knew the client on my table was integrating an internal healing that did not need to be fully revealed. Just the fact that they took time out of a busy schedule to lie down, strip away some of their defenses, expose their true face to someone else was a gift I never took lightly.

Our emotions can be carried on the surface for us to address like the skin. We can get a sense of these emotions felt on the surface throughout every day when we stay busy and try to ignore them. Too often, we hold emotions at a distance because we have judgments that they're not acceptable to us or to others around us. Do you steer clear of some emotions? We go to great lengths to hide or push away what we cannot accept, and just like the pimple that showed up on prom night, we can't find enough make-up to cover it up, though we try like hell!

In our recent history, we have come out of a two-year "lock-down" mode – a term previously used only for confinement in prisons. Such a mixture of emotions bottled up under pressure with too many questions to answer right out of the release. It is like a pimple on the face of a world that is not healing, and the pressure is building while our default action is to cover up and act like it's nothing to concern ourselves with. We are struggling to make sense of what has just run over us like a tsunami. Masks and our homes have become hiding places, and the built-up emotions denied and pushed away are not finding a place to be released. How long will this fester and stay inflamed? Can't we see and feel this pressure building? Is there a quick fix? Do we really have to look at ourselves in the mirror?

The silent fear of deeper conversations wants us to ignore connecting the dots and hope it will blow over – the IT becoming the pink elephant in the room. I've tried that technique, too.

The breakdown is brewing for a breakthrough. Can you feel it? What will it take to release the pressure so we can dive into the depths of this darkness to heal within? In my experience, there comes a time when we can no longer stay on the surface of ignoring and pushing down in denial even deeper. My journey gave that a great try.

If you look deep within yourself, you may find you have a journey within your own life of a part of you that you've "locked down" until the pressure was no longer bearable to sustain. A tired exhaustion to surrender was as much as you could offer to the world.

I went through a major life change about 25 years ago. I was living a life that I had built and followed in a direction that was very much to my mom's liking. She wanted me to live close to her, have a family to enhance family gatherings, be an upstanding person in our local church and community, and, as the only daughter, become the caretaker for my parents. I guess a part of me wanted that, too. It was easy enough to slide into, and many parts were very fulfilling. I deeply rooted myself in this life and became like others, living a life according to someone else's design.

Then things started to crumble. Has life crumbled for you, and all you can think about is "How can I patch this up so no one will notice?" I was doing this in so many directions that I didn't know when to stop until the therapist jarred me awake one session when she said, "You know you're married to an alcoholic, right? You know you're covering up his illness, right? You know this is destroying you, right?" Uh, no. I had no idea. That's not something I knew anything about. What the heck am I going to do with that?? No amount of make-up is going to cover that up!

Sometimes we have to look deeply at ourselves in the mirror, especially when we're crumbling, to see that the image we thought we were seeing (and living) was just a smoke and mirror trick to deceive us. I was covered in symbolic heavy-duty make-up that had its own addiction to try to please others so everything would look good. "SHIT!!" I don't want to look at this!! It must be the messed-up mirror – this can't be true!! I tried really, really hard not to see what was showing up (patchwork concealer to the rescue). The ugliness of my avoidance and unacceptance of myself and my life returned with even more cracks and was boldly staring back in my face.

Numbing and "busy-ness" could postpone it, I thought (heavier patch work). "Maybe I won't have to face this," or "Someone will fix it for me" were the consolations I offered myself for a moment of peace (patch, patch here … patch, patch there) – UNTIL my back was to the wall. Cornered in my own patchwork, I could not find the strength to look myself deep in the face, to let the ugly tears drain the wounds that were coming to the surface to be seen and wash away the concealer.

Layers had to fall away to allow the deeper hurts a place to release. I wanted to run away from the darkness within me, and I could not find a place to hide. All the beliefs I had told myself that life would be neat and tidy had to be seen in their illusion. I had put a lot of effort into keeping that concept alive. I threw lots of energy into looking good – trendy haircuts, yes, make-up, exercising, nice house, the list goes on – to support the life tied up with a neat bow. The magazines are filled with those images!

I'd tossed the coins into a deep well to appease Good Fortune and prayed never to personally have to dive down deeply within myself to realize all that I had tossed away: the shining bits of me that hold my true deep value. All of what I thought was my life collapsed. My marriage fell apart, my social network of friends turned their backs on me, my mom and I separated in disappointment.

A part of me was destroyed, and I can now realize that had to happen, that part of me had to let go: the part that was not really my true self. And because I had never previously journeyed outside of tending to others' lives and opinions, the idea of my true self was not even offered a space of "residence" within me. It was unthinkable to the mind of my dying self that I was actually in the process of becoming.

20/20 hindsight is elegant in its offering of valuable insight when you take the time, hold the courage, and stay in the willingness to be open to really see your raw self – the beliefs, the thoughts, the driving force that brings the action in life.

I had to face my shadow self, to feel deeply the remorse (and a wide assortment of other emotions) for choices I had made, and then to forgive myself and others. I had to hold responsibility by seeing that I had the ability and God-given right to respond in free will, and with that accept that I had made the choices and could move forward by learning. This inner perspective takes a lot of courage to explore, as well as loads of self-compassion.

I have come to appreciate the gifts of what I received during this time of chaos. I have grieved and still find waves of grief returning years later for the parts of me still being uncovered. There are aspects of me that grew and built strength, resilience, wisdom, courage, self-respect, self-love, self-trust, discernment, and so much more. By facing ourselves in the depth of love, we can remember more of our magnificence.

As my previous self collapsed, I found the strength to take one step at a time in new territory. I moved out of my small town into my own space. I learned that I could figure things out that I had never really given myself the opportunity to figure out before. My self-confidence grew. My self-respect grew. I grew... because I had a new conversation with myself. A courageous conversation that asked deeper questions to hear from deeper parts of me that had been stuffed away, with less concealing.

I found what it was like to please myself instead of everyone else. It took lots of falls to strengthen that muscle within me, because like a rubber band, old patterns have a strong gravitational pull to return to how they were before. And like so many shifts into awareness, life will keep offering you experiences to keep you committed to yourself. As you practice, there is less and less of a desire to return to the old patterns of that part that no longer serves you.

Perhaps some of my journey speaks to you. Perhaps you are starting to realize the image in the mirror you thought you'd see is not true – it is a made-up version that is concealed. Perhaps you find yourself holding your life together by running around patching up the cracks and hoping to cover-up or ignore what's crumbling because it's too scary to be in the unknowing, and it's damn messy. I know that part of you. I also somehow found a part within myself that could be a compassionate companion, especially at times when I didn't know which way to turn. Surprisingly, most of us have these parts in some version or another if we are willing to dive deep through the dark water of shame or fear to find our cast-off selves that are buried and waiting.

My journey continued to lighten up, the more I let go of the past parts of me that never fit. The gem I discovered about myself was that I was an avid learner when headed in the direction of my passion (what's in your heart). I moved to Maine so I could be in a healing place near water. Within months of moving, I learned about becoming an aesthetician and embraced every moment of learning, technique, and any testing that came my way. If I had not launched myself in a new direction, I would have died on the vine, like my therapist had warned.

There was an energetic flow (actually, it felt like a 2x4 whack on the head) that was pushing me in a different direction. The push was calling me to "get out of town" and be the brave, bold woman that needed to emerge. The key was my level of willingness. Oh, resistance was present, don't get me wrong. Heels were dug in deep. And I let go possibly more times than I could hold on. Was it a miracle? You bet. And we have them every day when we take one step to move on, just like Jesus walking on the water.

I ask you to come with me to take a look into the deep well of yourself. There is so much we have yet to uncover about ourselves, and no amount of concealer in the world needs to cover it up.

Why would one take that deep dive? Wouldn't it be easier to just float on the surface of life, numbing or avoiding? These are the questions we have to start asking ourselves each day, along with much deeper ones. The bigger the questions we ask, the bigger the answers. What seems clear to me is that the concealing idea was, and always has been, a really poor choice that is made by forgetting who we truly are.

Our forgetting distracts us into a dumbed-down state that has life leading us in others' directions rather than our own. Waking up from being hidden deeply under the covers is much tougher when there is an alarm shouting in your ears, and we are now recognizing that alarm is shouting very LOUD!

### Emotions the author experienced:

Feeling hollow, emptiness, betrayal, hope, compassion.

## Response to Maggie's Concealer

*by Owen*

Concealer.

Sometimes it comes in a bottle in the form of a liquid that I so intentionally apply to my aging face. Concealing the age spots and smoothing the lines that reveal my life's experiences.

As I continue to explore my concealer and where she applies, I am aware that she is the application of a careful blending and curating of what I think I can hide. What's curious about this is my ability to buy into it, at the moment. A smooth application of concealer and I am ready to face the day! (OMG are you kidding me!) "Fake it, till you make it!" – a motto applied to so many places in our culture. "Smile! You're on Candid Camera!" – implying that you never know where you might be caught on camera. (Terrifying if you think about it, and true in this day and age.)

If I dig deeper into the concealer or concealing patterns in my life – the ones that, at all costs, I don't want to fully feel – I notice the cover up and Band-aids that over time are worn away or washed away, leaving the truth in the mirror. Yup, the naked truth I have been hiding in the safety of my concealer.

Connecting with my concealing emotions has been a gift. It has been a permission slip in my life! It is my human right to have an experience of my emotions and to allow them to move through. When I consciously practice this, I notice the freedom and self-authority I have, which brings the resonance of love, joy, hope, and trust.

As Maggie so eloquently pointed to, our concealer is what keeps us from living our deepest, most exposed, rich life. It keeps us from dangerous emotions and the highest resonance of emotions, safe from feeling too much, allowing only the surface of emotions to be present.

**Emotions the author experienced:**

Love, joy, hope, trust.

## Naked on the Page

*by Owen*

Shattered.
Falling naked on the page.
Praying for my words,
chasing letters
for just the right one.

Always in
black and white
they slip
away.

Their hard edges,
angled lines
falling
against my soft,
supple breasts,
tired nipples,
scarred body
and burning heart.
Together we lie on the page.

Truth rolling out,
Messy, mired,
thickets and thorns
strewn across my backside.

I am just scratching
the surface,
with nails sharpened
and teeth baring –
My heart's been broken.

I lie awake exhausted,
my layers unfolding,
unbound and untethered.
The silence is screaming.

Teetering on the edges
of knives and lives –
mine of course,
who else?

The emotions
roll and roar
like bloodied battles,
emboldened,
embodied.

Stripped,
strangled
and static.
I pray –

Pray for
the parts of
myself
not yet born.

Yearning to emerge
with springs green,
fresh buds
and
clean, crisp air.

The water is waiting –
my board is perched,
calling me to
play.

Whispers and glimmers
of what awaits,
it promises to hold me
together
as we
heal.

**Emotions the author experienced:**

Rage, violence, anger, hope, compassion, love.

# EMOTIONAL CHECK-IN

What emotions arise when you think about showing your vulnerability?

When do you notice yourself putting up walls or masking your vulnerability?

What permission slip could you give yourself to let yourself be seen?

# Permission to feel "bad" emotions

## RAGE. HOPE. LOVE.

*by Owen*

I feel you creep in like fog on the water. Sometimes it's a slow drip, methodical and penetrating. Sometimes you body slam me, and I feel a shock, sick. You enter my belly, my chest and throat; my breath tightens, shortens, halting me. My mid-back and spine begin to buzz, heat penetrating my upper body. My neck and armpits sweat, my animal rising. A metallic taste in my mouth, seething saliva, tightening of my jaw, my sinuses activated and sharp.

The heat moves through me, I feel it behind my eyes and silencing my ears just for a moment. My hair at every follicle is ignited with fire, tingling, gripping, a rumbling volcano boiling inside me, lava ready to explode out.

I see you, I fear you, I love you. You are such a gift for me. You are MY RAGE!!

Hello RAGE!! You are my RAGE!! Shiny, sharp edges, sword-like, a firebomb!!

You are a gift to me – the recognition a boundary has been crossed, the clarity to move, change, and express my Rage. A gift that can feel dangerous. The danger lurks in not acknowledging and expressing you are here with me, inside me, whispering and yelling all at once. Rage, you are part of me.

How do we move together? Not to collude and shatter me, creating the separation that leaves me exhausted, lonely, and in deep despair.

Rage, I have come to welcome you. You are a pathway to hope and well-being. When we sit together and hold one another's hands, conscious of our breath and body temperature, we can see we don't need to blow up our world. We can express and feel the rage through yelling into a pillow and beating it, wringing a rag, throwing big rocks into the marsh, or yelling as loud as we can in the car.

Rage, you are often feared and deemed unacceptable. You are the depth of the darkest emotions most of us learn to dampen, numb out, or hide behind. You are feared as uncontrollable, and yet you bring wisdom and precision of energy that, when accessed, is powerful! For centuries people have tried to harness "a woman's rage." Yet it cannot be harnessed, bottled, and further abused – it is our personal power!! We all have it! You are a gift and a blessing! Listen to your rage; she holds magic, mystery, and love.

Sometimes our rage is best witnessed by a trusting friend to just hold the space, listen, be seen, be heard and acknowledged.

Using my voice, my words, my body to express rage.

From here, I get clarity and energy for movement. I can now see, feel, taste, and smell what needs to be tended to, spoken to, and addressed. Together we can find the hope and the love we truly seek.

Hope, for me, lands in my core, and I imagine my heart lights up! It has a special kind of trust and knowing that, although life may feel chaotic or in balance, my mattering is the place where hope resides.

Hope provides me with possibilities and wonder, a throughway to Love. I know you by the resonance in my body – warm, inviting, and full. The flow of energy I start to notice rising in my chest and gaze. My breathing is deep and full, filling my lungs, and I am able to exhale fully.

I notice the flow and ease when Hope rolls in. There is a sense that all is well in my body, my heart, and my soul. It's a beautiful launch pad to Love and well-being. Often when I feel Hope, Love is what's most present, sprinkling her sage and invitation. For when Love walks through my door, it's at once breathtaking, magical, and deeply humbling. OMG, Love. I get to feel you, be with you and experience a fullness like no other. It can send shivers through my body or a melty sensation like chocolate being poured over ice cream. My eyes soften, my body relaxes, and sometimes an excitement for Love energizes me and I am sure my feet aren't touching the ground.

The vibration starts in my belly and lady parts, moves right up my spine, and a glow with a glint in my eye emerges. Love, you are the elixir for what truly speaks to me and what scares the shit out of me. For Love, you can break my heart and grow it. To fully experience Love is vulnerable, and it's the gateway to more connection with my deepest desires and another's heart. Love is both kind and brutal; it lives with a light and a darkness like no other. Oh, how we are always looking for Love, and yet it's always here. In our soul's eyes gazing at us; in our heart's fiber, holding our hand and caressing each breath. Love.

**Emotions the author experienced:**

Rage, hope, love, sadness, violence, hopelessness,
despair, pity, overwhelm, grief.

## It Only Takes a Moment to Destroy a Lifetime of Building
*by Maggie*

The sword is swift
And the dying will be long
So, one is forced to feel the significance of the release ... that's the only thing present
The letting go of something or someone that seemed so closely bound.

We may think we did not see it coming – shock!

Yet we did ... EVEN if only a moment of a glimpse,
It registered a file of knowing of its coming, tucked away,
Denied its intent that it could really appear as it did.

And once the lethal wound struck the life, shock set in.
Feeling the process of it all slipping away,
The stages of begging to return to the way it was,
The agony and pain as the life path drips away,
The depth of remorse permeating every cell without escape.

You wanted it all to be different.
And the mind flashes the beautiful memories
That were held – convinced this would NEVER end –
This connection that was so different
And when held on its own, had the strength and conviction strong
enough to stand
the test of time
(Or so was thought).

Yet the outer world was set on destruction for its own sake.
Their strength was deeply rooted in generations,
Their mission had an ancestral cord,
With a grip tight to the sword, ready, waiting for the intruder they saw
as the enemy,
With their swing of the sword, a Judas-kiss whispered:
"We do this because we love you so."

**Emotions the author experienced:**

Hopelessness, despair, emptiness, feeling hollow,
revenge, hurt with betrayal, remorse.

# EMOTIONAL CHECK-IN

What do you feel about experiencing emotions like rage, violence, hatred, betrayal, and fury?

Which of these emotions are hardest for you to feel, and what messages shaped this?

What permission slip might support you in acknowledging and embracing feeling these emotions and the needs they are alerting you to?

# Permission to let it rip

## Rage that Takes Us Down

*by Maggie*

The rage I am feeling and have been feeling for over a week is building to such intensity in me. I want to scream and yell, "FUCK YOU!" at every moment. My body feels agitated, and my mind does not have the strength to focus. Everything in my way adds to the force of energy this holds within me. A bottle of catsup slips out of my hand as I get it out of the refrigerator. DAMN IT!! Now I've got that to deal with!!!

The rage continues, and I am thrown about in its fierceness and strength. Like a tiger on MY tail, I want to try to escape. This feels like I'm running for my life, with this pulsating energy that so wants to explode! My chest is pounding. I feel my heart rapidly reacting, even as the last of the catsup is wiped away. "Breathe," I tell myself. I sit on the floor with the catsup staining my hands, as there's too much to be cleaned up with the strength of the towel I grabbed. Somehow, sitting on the floor, I feel like I've hit a form of bottom, and I finally burst into tears with primal sobbing. Release. A draining of the wound I've tried so hard to control and contain. It's out of its cage, and the sobs grow stronger and uncontrolled. "I'm a mess. My life is a mess!!," I hear inside my head.

Nothing like my inner critic to kick me when I'm down! The sobs take my breath away. I am at their mercy. A heap of a woman feeling such deep pain and despair drenched in catsup on the floor is such a contrast to who she can be. Who am I in the truest sense of this being? How can such a contrast be the same person living and breathing in the same body, with the same face, hands, feet? Who the FUCK am I really? My mind opens me to curiosity, if even for a moment, that shifts the intense emotion of rage into confusion and doubt, and for some reason these emotions seem a bit of a relief from the "I'll take you down!" rage that had been building like an unattended fire within me.

With a moment or two of relief, I catch my breath, and with that breath I offer a deeper breath that fills and soothes a part of me that was ready to bust. I bring myself back into a partial awareness of where I am and what's on the floor beside the catsup. I feel a sense of a nurturing presence within me, as if she's laying a hand on my back – gently, calming. I take another breath, deep and filling.

I know the higher, truer self as an amazing, beautiful, wise, loving, caring woman. I wonder how that part of me could be taken down by a thought that didn't even originate with me. What I'm coming to know about the human psyche is that we are multi-faceted, with many parts operating under the same "roof," so to speak. As I connect with this present feeling, I become more aware that a part of her (me) bought into a lie that someone had shared about her – A FUCKING LIE!!! Yet the damage this Little One was feeling was her deep wound that she was wrong, and anything that stuck to that wound, even if it was a lie, could reignite and trigger it.

The clarity and the self-compassion that was starting to be heard in my head was a far cry from the profane, explosive, raging demon I heard within me only moments before. This emerging voice of observation looked at the catsup-stained towel, saying almost with a reframe, *I'm right here for you, Love. I can sit with you in catsup on the floor, just as well as I can be at your side when your confidence in yourself returns. I'm right here.*

I could feel my body, especially my shoulders, soften. I could feel the sting from crying, soothed. I could now open up to another layer of compassion for the part of me that had just returned from such an emotional rollercoaster of an experience. I felt myself become limp. My mind symbolized the towel as me, and like the towel could not hold all the catsup. I, too, could not, nor did I want to, hold someone else's baggage of lies and shame that was thrown on me. The sting was present, though the healing had begun. I felt my whole body ache from the engagement of this emotion ravishing through me, taking me down, when a vulnerable part of me was not strong enough on her own to face this wave of shame.

My primary self, the part of me that KNOWS her truth, had been missing in action, away from the driver's seat of my life. No wonder this rage had taken such hold! My Little One felt and was in the line of fire and unprotected by me – and it all sparked in a moment. When the Little One feels abandoned, our body can feel it. Our parts are such great teachers for us, though unless we pay attention to this miraculous, multifaceted aspect of ourselves, we miss the great healing and growing potential we have in life.

Emotions are the very essence of our daily living, yet they often go undiscovered, or we are unwilling to get to know them. At this time, I was running away from my rage – not wanting to face it, to get to know this essential part of myself. It is a form of disassociation. I feared and lacked the respect that this emotion could offer me.

Little did I realize at the time that under all this intense present-day feeling was my Little One frozen in memory, who was told by the outside world that she was in trouble and bad. She didn't know how to stand up for herself. She didn't know how to feel the hurt and pain that others tried to inflict on her, and so her fear just kept building and building until everything was at the point of breaking. And the beauty of it all was ... she didn't break.

How can you begin to recognize and feel your emotions?

Emotions are an energy of awareness. It takes only a moment to check in with yourself, to start a process of connecting to your emotions and realize they are normal.

I've learned a practice to have daily check-ins, either with myself or with a partner. It only takes a few moments to name and verbalize the emotions that are present. That recognition, with an acceptance that all emotions are normal and part of our humanness, allows space to breathe into, instead of shutting it down, or numbing it out, or dealing with it another, more "convenient" time.

It always amazes me how quickly any emotion will subside and flow when we take the time to be with it (scientifically, it takes about 2 ½ minutes, maximum). After that short moment you can journal about it, name it to a friend (the story of it is best left untold), beat the ground with a towel (the Earth can dissipate it), or find other inventive ways to respond to what comes up. It is in the addressing of the emotion (being willing) – feeling that it (and you) matter/s – that opens the natural flow and motion.

Lately I have had great results with Biofield Tuning, which I have found to be helpful for recognizing emotions stuck within me. If you have not tried naming your emotions or even getting familiar with them, I highly encourage you to start. Not only does this awareness offer valuable insight to you and your amazing multi-faceted parts, it also allows a time, space, and technique for emotions to return to flow within you and your life. The flow can bring us back to the alignment of our original operating system.

We are now discovering that when emotions do not flow, energetic blockages in the body and the biofield (a measurable field 6-7 feet surrounding the physical body) vibrate with frequencies that were previously undetected without frequency tools. We are designed for emotional energy to flow. Sometimes, simple physical acts such as walking, being in nature, and pleasure (to name a few) can return the flow, though our stressed-out world has locked us down to avoid addressing our emotions. That puts "kinks" of sorts in our light body system, and we can dim or shut down. We then feel shut down mentally, physically, and emotionally.

How do we return to the original operating system and flow? You can start by recognizing what parts and emotional blockage you have that are being called out to be healed. We are now aware of the inner damage this blockage can cause (since energy can never be destroyed). So, I invite you to take steps to connect to your emotions. In shifting your awareness, your willingness, self-love, and a few moments of your time, you can shift your world. I know you're worth it!

### Emotions the author experienced:

Rage, despair, anxiety, abandonment, worthlessness, compassion.

## Sadness
*by Owen*

"You seem sad," someone said. "I am," I whispered as tears welled in my tired eyes. I am in a pool of Sadness, surrendered to my being and feeling deeply. A deep well of sorrow and heartache.

Today I am here to speak of Sadness. It lands in my body and feels so heavy, I wonder if it's something else. Nope, it's Sadness – my heart is aching. I have been resisting being in my Sadness, as it brings with it a flood of emotions and rivers of tears. Well, here we are, tears flowing, Sadness rolling, and my body aches with heat. Ahh, sweet sorrow, and the prick of a rose thorn reminds me I am alive. This is a new Sadness, with flavors of past and newly present sadness. I have filled my coffers, and they are overflowing. A tide rising.

It's OK, I hear whispered to me from afar, You aren't going to die or lose everything. You are sitting in the spectacular, magnificent Sadness of being.

There is nowhere to go, to hide or cover up – it's calling me to rest and close my eyes. I am Sadness. My chest is heavy, my eyes hurt, and my breath is slow.

Sadness has brought with it Hopelessness and Despair, with a flavor of Pity and Overwhelm. I sit with Sadness, and together we experience one another and notice the commitment to swim in this pool. In this pool, there is no time limit or drain for which to pull the plug – there is only a ladder in the distance, waiting for when I am ready to climb out. The Sadness holds my Grief, which feels like the raft I am floating on. This is the Grief that can hold me while I rest on her, floating in this pool.

*Be in the Sadness*, I hear, as I dive under the Grief to see the glimmers of Rage, Violence, and Hope.

Ahh, Hope, there you are, like a beautiful aquamarine stone shining at the bottom. I reach for you. I am not able grab to you yet, but I feel you in my heart –

Shining your blue light. Reminding me I am alive.

**Emotions the author experienced:**

Sadness, hopelessness, despair, pity and overwhelm, grief, rage, violence, hope.

# EMOTIONAL CHECK-IN

What do you feel about the idea of safely letting your emotions rip in an intentional way?

In what ways do you currently express or suppress your emotions, and how does that impact you?

Is there a permission slip you could give yourself to safely and intentionally release your emotions?

# Permission to feel shame

**Shame**

*by Owen*

"SHAME ON YOU...!"

Words I heard often as a child. Sometimes it was the dog who had rolled in something gross and my father, angry, would shame the dog. "SHAME ON YOU!!!" I remember him saying these words to my younger brother and me at the tender ages of 4 and 2, or 5 and 3 – too young to understand what we had done, but old enough to understand the tone and the anger that brought on such damaging words. Words that wound over time, like little cuts on our little selves. I have locked this feeling of BEING ASHAMED in my body. It starts in my gut and rolls up my back to the back of my neck and throat; it's warm and filled with tension. My ears sometimes hurt.

It has taken a lot of self-reflection and mining to understand that the shame is not mine. I remember when I first learned about shame and was taken through a process to release it and hand it back. I was in disbelief. How could this be possible?! My younger selves believed wholeheartedly that I was to be ashamed and stay there forever more. Shame gets locked in. For me it came with fear, anxiety, and confusion and meant that I was bad – in fact, very bad!

What's curious is that as I have healed and nurtured the younger parts of myself that experienced this kind of shame, I have let go of the story. What stayed as a reminder are the words, the body sensation, and the knowing that the shame I was once burdened with is not mine!! Even as I write this, I can feel my throat tense, and the saliva in my mouth feels warm. I take a breath, and even with the healing and mastery of emotional work I have done, I still remember the feeling of shame.

Emotions the author experienced:

Shame, hurt, blame, anger.

## Acceptance and Shame
*by Holly*

There is a part of me I need to look at. A part of me in shame. I have walked away, cut ties with my mother and sister. This is, in most people's eyes, an unusual thing to do. Meghan Markle was slammed for it by Piers Morgan on Good Morning TV in the UK. He suggested that her pattern was to cut and run. I resonate with her choice, understand it, and feel furious and a little intrigued by what he said. I look into myself.

Come forward, my hurt and shamed parts, tell me of your story and how it felt for you, and reclaim the pieces of you that are being hidden away. The ones that I avoid telling people about in order to avoid their judgment, questions, and sometimes lectures. Come forward, and do not say how bad your life was and justify your choice. Come forward instead to say, "I am okay with this. This was the right choice for me. This was what I needed." In complete compassion for both yourself and those involved.

I heal my shame by handing it back to those who choose to shame me. Here's a journal extract that shows how I have been doing that:

*Dear Little Self,*

*You thought you had to stay with the craziness and the abuse. I wish I could have been there to save you. You lost your childhood to fear. You didn't get to play.*

*Now I'm grown up, I can say to you I wish you had run away or told a teacher, because then everything could have come out. Maybe you would have felt safer in the world. More supported. Held less shame.*

*Just like you, I don't know that. We can't say for sure that it would have been better. However, there may have been a possibility of things being better. That's a risk worth taking. If not, at least you tried. You lost nothing.*

*You already faced the worst, Little One. You were and are so brave. And now I'm here to ask you to take my hand, let me walk with you as you escape that tortured place. You no longer have to remain here.*

*I wish to steady your heart as you make courageous choices. The choice to live. The choice to be wild and free. The choice to be responsible. The choice to experience joy and love.*

*You've got to operate differently, make different choices, if you want to get different results.*

*In the past, you chose to stay in an unhealthy environment, to change your soul in a fruitless attempt to experience love.*

*What choices do you want to make now instead?*

*I choose to seek healthy environments where safety, love, and compassion abound.*

*I choose to protect myself and remove myself from unhealthy people and places.*

*I choose to retreat, even run, from danger. I can't fight all these dragons alone. I don't even want to fight. I choose to lay my weapons down and focus on creating peace.*

*There is always the possibility of harmony, if you let yourself flow to and with it.*

*Be at peace, Little One.*

*Trust your own heart.*

*Release the critic who says you are not enough, for discerning that it's a poisoned environment.*

*Flowers can't grow in poisoned soil.*

*You may clean up the soil if it's within your gift to do so. Or you simply keep moving, until you find fertile ground in which to plant your seeds.*

*I thought I needed more courage. It turns out I just needed to give myself permission. Permission to run away to more fertile ground. Permission to trust and follow my heart, without making myself wrong or bad for it.*

*It's time to drop the belief that I am wrong. That core moment in my wounding logic. I recall being six and thinking everyone around me can't be wrong; it must be me that's wrong.*

*It turns out they could all be wrong. When your immediate surroundings are filled with deeply wounded others, that's exactly how it is. You can be right, even though they're all saying you're wrong.*

*Wounded people attract other wounded people. I was surrounded by wounded people and backwards logic. I adopted their ideals as my own, in order to fit in and find love. In order to survive.*

*All the while cutting myself off from the true source of love. The love in my own heart for my soul, for who I am.*

*It does not matter if others love you or not. It matters that you love yourself, care for yourself, protect yourself.*

*You can do it.*

*And when you do, oh, how powerful you will truly be, as nothing can take that loving acceptance and trust away from you.*

*With this came the realization: I can't live my mother's dream.*

*What I have come to see is that my mother sacrificed certain things for me to have the privileges I have. She knew that a good education, something she didn't have, was a path to a better life. I am so grateful she instilled this in me and supported it happening for me.*

*At the same time, that vision of a better life was a Boomer's vision. Earning more, living lavishly, having security, and so on. That's what my mother wanted for me – what she never had. This was her dream, though, not mine.*

*So, when I quit the safe and well-paid corporate job that was slowly draining my soul of all life, to her it seemed as if I was throwing it all away. A kick in the teeth, one could say, after all she had sacrificed. She certainly let me know she thought I was stupid and "crazy" to give it up.*

*I longed for her to be one of those parents who just wanted their kids to be happy. I felt my mother wanted me to be successful, even at the cost of my mental health and well-being. I just wanted to feel some joy and meaning in my life. My dream was and still is to have a joyful and meaningful life.*

*My mother's actions taught me that my dream was not enough for her. I was not acceptable to her. I was accused of judging her, when I wasn't. I was happy for her to have her own dream, and I asked her to be respectful of mine. To stop saying I was lazy and a fool to leave that job, and instead celebrate with me, because it was one of the things I am most proud of in my life.*

*It took a lot to give up privileges and follow where my soul was guiding me. My mother couldn't understand how such privileges could bring me down. I was called self-centered and entitled. I was even cut off from support and connection. I make up that this was an attempt to "kick me into reality," as my mother would say. To make me realize I needed to be responsible for myself and not be lazy and entitled.*

*Instead of causing me to U-turn, I felt into the rejection, abandonment, and fear. "You're on your own now, Holly. It's up to you what you make of this life," I thought. I was beset with feeling worthless, abandoned, powerless, and lost. At the same time, I was free to pursue my well-being, develop a sense of self and purpose, and be responsible for the choices I would make. And that was thrilling.*

*Unfortunately, this gap in world views has, so far, been too big for my mother and me to bridge. I had peered into the world of riches, had experiences my mother could have only dreamed of at my age. She wanted that for herself, and she couldn't understand how I could walk away from it all.*

*I needed to walk away from the so-called "great job" because I so thoroughly believe that my actions have consequences on our world. It was born out of a deep responsibility I felt to ensure that humans create a world where all life can thrive.*

*My version of success was to have enough to live, and to do something about the fact that our world is on fire in every way – socially, environmentally, politically. Our systems are failing to sustain life for the future, and I wanted to do something about it. I also wanted to be passionate, creative, and playful.*

*Having experienced a deep wound of rejection through my mother, I was being sabotaged by my inner grapples. I didn't feel like I was enough. Maybe I was lazy and entitled? Am I depressed? Why, oh why, couldn't I just get on with it and suck it up like generations before me? Was I expecting too much? Who am I to believe I can create what I want to experience in the world?*

*I didn't know if I could change the world, but I knew I could change me. So that's what I did. I dedicated myself to figuring out how to feel* free and worthy enough to follow my dreams, how to accept who I am, and how to love myself enough to believe in myself and my dreams.

I have always been a dreamer and an optimist. I recall feeling terribly hurt by a co-worker in my graduate job who told me that I was too idealistic. He was right, I am idealistic, and today I am proud of that. It takes a very strong person to hold hope for a better world. I'd rather do that than abandon myself and turn my hope into pessimism or suppressed rage.

All of my deepest, darkest emotions were guiding me to my gifts, idealism and hope being some of them. Hold on to your hope and ideals, I say, and love yourself even when others project advice from a place of having given up on their dreams in order to fit in and belong.

Ultimately, my emotional journey has been about learning to belong to myself, because no one can ever take that away from me. I choose to stop abandoning my desires, dreams, and preferences, and start listening to them. I choose to take a stand for believing in myself, even when no one else does.

Now I've chosen my role in life to be that person who shows others how to believe in yourself when no one else does. When advocates, activists, artists, change-makers, idealists, innovators, entrepreneurs, and many others need a direction to channel their energy, I say: find a mission. Take the unconventional path, not the one society and anyone else expects of you. Find that meaningful pursuit that gives your life purpose and fulfillment, no matter whether you achieve the outcome or not. You are enough, and you are worthy of love for being who you are. Be the you who is unchanged by external circumstances.

Practicing being courageous enough to be emotionally authentic has helped me redefine my story, claim my strength and power, and make my life and work an expression of my love and joy. I'm human. Like anyone else, I have my downward spirals and make mistakes. I also bring myself through them by going with the flow of my emotions, not against it.

Practicing feeling all of my emotions with total acceptance has taught me that they always take us on a journey back to our most authentic self and beyond surviving to thriving.

I lost my mother and gained myself and the hope of a brighter world.

**Emotions the author experienced:**

Abandonment, rejection, hurt, grief, shame, blame, sadness, compassion, hope, joy, passion, self-authority, well-being, thrill.

# EMOTIONAL CHECK-IN

What emotions do you feel when you consider that shame can mask other feelings?

In what ways does shame block you from fully experiencing or expressing your true emotions?

Is there a permission slip you could give yourself to acknowledge and release shame?

# Permission to be perfectly imperfect

## School

*by Owen*

Oh, shit!! My heart begins to race, and I can feel my younger self wanting to hide, recede, separate, and disappear. The emotions of fear, terror, despair, and abandonment run through my chest and upper back, my face gets red, and I begin to sweat. The part of me that speaks and expresses herself with her art, and the learned listening to articulate her voice, has not had the courage to allow her voice to hit the page. WORDS!! IN BLACK AND WHITE!! Fuck, Fuck, Fuck! ... SHIT! And then just as I reach this edge, I hear the softness, the anchored, knowing voice calling me back to the present with warmth and grace, with an offer to breathe, be still. A hand reaching out, resting between my shoulder blades, a knowing glance with deep love and honor, asking me to trust, and so I trust.

*Trust me, I've got you! I love you!*

*I want you to feel me, know me, as I stand with a hand on your back. Stay in the presence of my voice – it's clear, conscious, and loved.*

This is the younger voice I have kept inside for a very long time. I feel her in my heart when I listen deeply, a quiet, soft presence. Her only ask is to be seen and heard. She is the most tender, sensitive voice, the one who just knows! The one who feels deeply, sees and senses with her body and soul.

My heart aches often with the voice of rage and violence, boiling in the learned conditions to stay quiet and safe. I am the cool voice that rolls in with the clarity of hard truth. I am loud and clear. The safety is in the chaos I cannot tame.

I am here to tell you it's OK to let the rage and violent words out on the page. Feel them, name them, and know they serve you as they hit the page. They are deep. Sweet one, they are the shadow to the love and grace you share in the world, the paradox of emotions we all carry. It's all welcome. My longing for you is to know you are loved and all your emotions belong. In the deepest, tenderest of places with few words lives your true essence. It's the color of the calm oceans that at times rage, or the setting red sun with its mystery of darkness, and upon us a moon-lit sky shines on.

Dear one, you are magnificent. Your sensitive soul has a voice that longs to be written. Your experience in school over the years shamed your spelling and missed the mark. An unfurling of terror and error, as you trip your way through a system of learning that leaves you feeling abandoned and lonely. The letters and symbols don't make sense when put together on the page, they are unfamiliar and confusing. The times you can put your words on paper – and, God willing, they happen to make sense and line up – are a win. A win that is short and often followed with another page marked in red and circled with comments. The markings only bring shame, even when the teacher writes, "Good job!!" It all falls into the hole of unworthiness and loneliness.

You see, dear one, you are a good listener! In fact, it's your superpower – you just can't read and write like the others. Over time you are taken out of classes and given extra help which comes with the experience of separateness, and the emotions of hopelessness and despair. You abandon yourself, and overwhelm rolls in. Your face turns red when you are asked to read aloud. Inside you're screaming, "I don't know how. I can't see how. This is meaningless." You are filled with blame and betrayal, only 5, 7, and 9, then 11. The rage and hatred toward yourself for not being able to keep up, stay in the lane, retain the words as they were meant to be written. Learning along the way to cope and sometimes make shit up that works.

You work hard at school and often barely get by. The only one in your family with this kind of learning style, the others make it look easy. And to them, it is. They don't understand, and your confusion becomes theirs. The frustration and despair make doing the work a nightmare. They try to help, and fights ensue, as your shame is deep and rage is true. "Why can't I get it right?" "What's wrong with me?" Oh, sweet one, there is absolutely nothing "wrong" with you. As you later come to find out, your brain is wired a little differently.

You hide and find ease in the big, red "C" on your paper. You make peace with it, befriend it. It belongs to you!! The quiet voice inside you longs for more, hears more, sees more, and experiences the rainbow of love that comes from within when creating with your hands. Your essence, my love, is tender and sweet, kind and loving, fierce and knowing. You MATTER!!

Over time, you quietly embrace your itching hands and creative spaces to explore and express what the written words cannot.

This becomes your safe space, a place to retreat, a place to soar, dream, be, and land in your tender heart. Hand-stitching buttons on your favorite blanket at 5, learning to knit at 7, teaching yourself to use the sewing machine at 8, and taking ballet and modern dance along the way. You see, dear one, expression comes in so many forms, and they aren't always words on the page.

In 8th grade, your father, at the recommendation of the director of the Boston Children's Museum, decides to explore getting you tested and then hires a tutor in dyslexia. This is the doorway to healing your shame and hopelessness. With this tutor, you begin to rewire your brain, expose the coping mechanisms, and see a path forward. It comes in the whispers and tears of letting go of the "C" you came to love.

This is a vulnerable time. You have to trust, be patient, and receive – receive the help that for so long felt foreign and terrifying. You have to forgive yourself and eventually those closest to you for their lack of understanding.

For we were all in the dark. As the land of language and words begins to mend, click, line up, flow, your body begins to relax and recognize the symbols and sounds. The words could be yours, like the color combinations in your 80s outfits.

The "C" becomes a marker in time and the place you find safety. It means you passed and didn't fail; it's your comfort zone, reliable. You find ease in the rewiring and recognition. The speed at which you catch up and pivot towards the journey that eventually leads you to this place is quite exquisite. It brings you hope, optimism, and satisfaction – all of them new emotions for school.

By the time you are 17, you have embraced a fierce, raw, passionate nature that is unstoppable. You graduate high school in the 11th grade and head off to art school in NYC. Here you find others who see like you, listen like you, and have words like you. This brings peace and freedom, a sense of belonging.

After two years, you transfer to the Rhode Island School of Design, finding your place in the world of threads and textiles. Designing and creating fabric allows you to bridge the gap of language, math, and design, becoming more whole. The literal weaving together of patterns and shapes designed with math and designated letters makes complete sense to you now. You feel the freedom of individuality, passion, and the thrill of standing in your self-authority and creating!! This presence is honored by your professors and future employers. Your voice matters!!

Dear one, you are in your rightful place and honored. You are seen and heard, and the language of art and design becomes your place of mastery. The "C" becomes the lint in your pocket to the "A" you now create. Allow this to sink in and filter through your body; experience authority, joy, love, passion, and freedom!! The excitement and thrill of completion and success.

Fast forward to your youngest daughter, who is in first grade and the teacher pulls you aside to share her worry: Lucy is confusing her letters and can't seem to read. You masterfully and knowingly see what's here, Lucy has some of you. She is dyslexic.

This part of you that has been one of your biggest gifts and a source of great confusion and pain. You are a powerful Mama Bear who rolls in and understands immediately what is needed. Help!

As you step into your role as nurturing parent and advocate, accepting and knowing the road will be challenging, there are so many emotions, not the least of which is grief. This sits heavy in your heart and comes with such sadness and despair of your younger selves – the parts that still need to be healed. Oh, sweet one, this is a gift, an opportunity for you to receive and be for Lucy what you had to wait to experience. Nurturing.

Together, you and Lucy navigate this next chapter by embracing and leading with your tender, wise heart. You are activated, a heightened sensitivity rolls in, knowing that Lucy's journey of dyslexia is hers. You manage to find your old tutor who has been running a business for decades in the next town over. You notice the coincidence and get in touch.

Over the next five years, Lucy will be provided with a language and math tutor. Lucy will voice the things you never said out loud, she will honor you with her tears of frustration and rage. You will honor her with your knowing and love. Together, you have this!! The full circle of dyslexia has honored you. It has not been an easy road, but it's one that feels true.

You are a good mother, dear one, a conscious fierce loving mother!! It's an honor to witness you.

### Emotions the author experienced:

Fear, terror, despair, abandonment, rage, violence, loneliness, blame, compassion, self-authority, frustration, despair, trust, hope, love.

# EMOTIONAL CHECK-IN

What emotions do you feel around embracing your imperfections?




In what areas of your life do you feel pressure to be perfect, and how does that affect you?




What permission slip could you give yourself to accept and celebrate your imperfections?

# *Permission to love imperfectly*

## The Imperfect Parent

*by Marna*

It is 3 am, and I'm wide awake.

The usual nagging, worried thought has awoken me: I'm failing my kids.

This worry quickly turns to anxiety as I imagine the future playing out, given the trajectory we're on. Panic sweeps in, then gives way to frustration and helplessness because I "know" how I wish to be in relationship with my kids – I want to parent them from love and connection, rather than fear, anger, and separation – but I just keep reacting without remembering this. It feels impossible to break out of this deep rut, yet I am desperate to do so!

The daily battles with my youngest are where I feel the most desperate. I am continually blindsided by how a seemingly mundane request or a perfectly reasonable "No" from me can send my youngest child into a rage. It feels like I'm suddenly tossed overboard and am grasping for any tactic that might pull me out from the stormy seas: Demanding. Reasoning. Sympathizing. Distracting. Threatening. Bargaining.

But none of it ever works! He shuts me down every time because he is wise to our dance. He will not be convinced, manipulated, or controlled. I feel trapped, held hostage by his unyielding resistance every time.

I keep getting sucked into an undertow of blame: *Why is he doing this to me? Why is he so damn stubborn? I'm trying so hard to do all the right things to be a good parent! Why does he insist on making my life so hard?*

I've read so many parenting books, desperately searching for strategies to be calm, prevent his meltdowns, or effortlessly navigate them ... but I can't find the right answers for our situation or master any technique fast enough before I'm back in it again! I feel completely lost at sea, like I'm being tossed about in the waves, flailing and hollering ... until I finally just give up, stop pushing, and allow myself to sink, surrendering to it all. Only then do I manage to see him as a human being who is struggling to get his voice heard, to have his agenda matter, to get his needs met ... like me. I somehow find my footing and get out of the water, and my child and I find a way to move on.

Too often, though, that doesn't happen until after I've modeled unhelpful and unhealthy communication of anger, or I've made him wrong for his developmentally age-appropriate behavior, or I've shut down out of frustration, turning away and withdrawing in some way because I feel that familiar dark rage called apathy settling in (*Nothing I'm doing is making a difference. What's the point in engaging?*).

Here, in the darkness, the pain of these repeated ruptures in our relationship, and the knowledge that I'm the one creating them, causes my heart to break ... and then grief pours in for the relationship I longed to have with him.

I sob in frustration and despair, "Why does this have to be so hard!? Why can't I get my parenting 'shit' together?! Why can't I just be the calm, compassionate parent I'm supposed to be, that I need to be, that he needs me to be? What's wrong with me?!" The tears continue until I have nothing left, and I lay there, exhausted.

In the silence that follows, I feel a compassionate presence waiting to pull me in and whisper words of comfort. I grab my journal and let the words pour out of me:

*My Love,*

*I see you there, carrying so much heartbreak, frustration, humiliation, and shame over the way you keep showing up as a parent.*

*You never, in your wildest imagination, could've known it would be this hard, this unrelenting, this overwhelming, this isolating. You are parenting two young, energetic, and complex kiddos, and now in a pandemic. You are swimming in a vast sea of uncertainty. It is TERRIFYING having so little control. And it also feels enraging to be sold this Giant Lie that we can and should control our children – and that their compliance proves our success and worthiness as parents.*

*I feel how angry you are – it's so unfair that you weren't taught how to parent in a calm, compassionate, connected way! It's so unfair that you weren't shown how to lean in and get curious when your children aren't behaving in the way you expect. It makes sense that you're angry! And it makes sense that, when you're under so much stress, you respond in the way you learned: you turn away in impatience, frustration, and bafflement, and shut down.*

*And I feel your rage... You repeatedly seek out support, but it does not show up in the way you need. You feel dismissed, minimized, abandoned, betrayed, and completely alone.*

*I want you, dear one, to know you're not alone.*

*You're not the only one who is moved quickly from impatience to frustration and blame when things aren't going the way you expect them to.*

*You're not the only one who loses it and yells at their kids.*

*You're not the only one whose kids are afraid of them from time to time.*

*You're not the only one who is struggling to find time alone to breathe, regroup, re-center.*

*AND YET, here you are, so deeply committed to forging a new path, to finding a new way to parent that's rooted in love and connection, not fear and control.*

*You keep showing up, every single day, ready to try again.*

*You keep seeking out help and support.*

*You are on the right path, and you are taking steps forward every single day.*

*I want you to know that I see you.*

*I see how hard you're working to make a more loving, understanding, and deeply connected relationship with your kids than you had.*

*I want you to know that you are not failing, dear one.*

*You are not a failure.*

*You care. You care with all of your being.*

*These relationships matter to you.*

*These humans matter to you.*

*And that's why when you make a mistake, you regroup, you take in some big breaths,*

*and you head back out there to make it right.*

*You get down to their level, you lean in with love, you admit your mistake, you apologize.*

*You ask for a re-do.*

*You really listen to what they want and need, and you find a way through that feels right to both of you.*

*All of this new terrain in parenting is being forged by you, one moment at a time.*

*And the journey is fueled by your desire to create the kind, compassionate world you want to see.*

*These moments of rising up, feeling it all, welcoming in compassion – the trying again, "This time with a little more love" is what's important.*

*There is SO MUCH to celebrate in that.*

*You are doing a heroine's work.*

*You are here, on this earth, at this time, to create deep, meaningful relationships rooted in the belief that people MATTER.*

*I can feel your passion welling up in you now, your deep commitment stirring to make this so.*

*You show people they matter because you keep showing up.*

*You show yourself that you matter because you keep showing up.*

*You keep showing up again and again, against all odds, facing storm after storm after storm. You never give up.*

*You let people know that they are still loved, even with their storm clouds.*

*Well, my dear, you are loved with all of yours.*

*Your storm clouds are big because you care so much.*

*Permission to bring whatever weather you have.*

*You. Are. Loved. No. Matter. What.*

*Permission to parent, dear one, just as you are.*

**Emotions the author experienced:**

Frustration, resentment, blame, shame, desperation and panic, apathy, helplessness, compassion, love, relief, remorse, self-blame, anxiety, compassion, love, forgiveness, self-authority, trust, hope.

## Motherhood

*by Owen*

Motherhood
I'll say it again
MOTHERHOOD!

It's a landscape
Full of cracks
Clanging bells
Splinters wood and steel
Shards and shattered windows
Cookies and cakes
Creepy crawlers
Deep wells and
Oceans of love
Krispy treats
Mud pies
Love muffins
And ...... SHIT!

MOTHERHOOD!
I'll say it again
MOTHERHOOD!
Comes with so many moments
To fall
To rise
To befriend

To be fired
To lose
To find freedom
To go unconscious and numb
To love so deeply you think
OH MY GOD I MIGHT DIE!
It's uncharted, and there is no map
We create it as we go
Bringing our best
And our worst
Celebrating with,
but often not ourselves
For being imperfect and
uniquely original
And magnificent.

Motherhood
I'll say it again
MOTHERHOOD!

I am not my mother…
For my mother is "Perfect"
Shattered
Adored
Shamed
Admired
Selfless
Selfish
Sexy
Shy
Lovely
Lonely
Loving
Lost
Freedom to love

Found and forgotten
Making a map
I can't be her map,
It doesn't fit
My compass is
My own
She is 5'7
I am 6'0
She is birdlike,
I am a bear

Motherhood
I'll say it again
MOTHERHOOD!

We seek
We shame
We love
Too much, too little
Too late
We hate and blame
Disconnected

Only to connect
Like ties on a dress
About to come apart,
We hold and tend
To others before ourselves

When in fact we ache
To be seen for
Who we really
Are –
MOTHERS.

Mothers.
I'll say it again,
MOTHERS.
We come with strings
And stings
The shoulds
And shouldn'ts.

The lies
We believe until
We surrender
Into the unknown

Allowing the threads
Of our mothers
To ride alongside
Beloved and betrayed
Bestowed

Acceptance
I'll say again,
ACCEPTANCE...
The beautiful imperfect
Perfect mother
In you!

What if you celebrated?
Ate your cake
And changed diapers
Loved and laughed

All while crying
Because
Some days
Are

Messy and missing,
Broken
And lost at sea.

What if we accepted?
Our mothers
Our ties and knots
Accepted ourselves
With our fresh-bruised hearts
And babies' new skin
Accepted for our beauty
Our grace
Our grit
Our imperfect way to love
And be loved

What if we accepted
Just ourselves?
Our being.
Perhaps
First with hesitation
Then recognition
And
Ahh, there you are!
Love!
We accept LOVE!
It's not dressed up
Or down.

It's always with you
Perhaps a whisper
Or the soft air
Shifting.
Take a breath
Receive

Love!

Love
I'll say it again
LOVE!!
ENOUGH
LOVE
ENOUGH
LOVE.

Mom, you are Love.
Mom, I am Love.

A Mother's Love.

**Emotions the author experienced:**

Love, freedom, shame, loneliness, betrayal, acceptance.

# EMOTIONAL CHECK-IN

What emotions do you feel in relation to loving imperfectly, whether in intimate or family relationships, friendships, or with yourself?

Where do you notice the most pressure to love or care for others perfectly, and how does that affect you?

Is there a permission slip you could give yourself to love in a more imperfect yet authentic way?

# Permission to choose love

## Choose Love

*by Holly*

Love, like all emotions, is a choice. We don't think it's a choice – we think feelings arise in us and just happen to us. Yet today I know my feelings are a choice, a vibration I choose to hold and embody.

Choice. I didn't always think love was a choice. I chose to love. Love didn't flow back to me. So, I got confused. All I ever wanted was to feel loved. For someone to choose to love me. Forever. Love left me, I thought.

Everyone who loves me leaves me. That was my script. The inevitable ending to all my desires, that was pre-set in the past. Inherited from the stories of my ancestors. My family forgot how to love. I lacked love, and I was unlovable.

Each child being desperate for the experience of being loved began seeking this wondrous experience. In seeking to get love, they couldn't choose love. They chose to experience themselves as an empty cup.

Where does one find love? In the depths of one's own heart. The confusion was, I have no love. No, my dear, you have love – you were looking for confirmation from the outside world of the love that's inside you.

Unfortunately, the environment you grew up in was filled with grown-ups who also believed they lacked love. Were unlovable. They were so busy seeking it outside of themselves that they forgot they had love inside too.

We all forget we have a choice. To choose to feel love and to love. No matter what occurs in the outside world, you are lovable. Like the seed is initially flowerless, but not empty. You are a filled-up cup of love potential waiting to blossom.

If you choose to believe it, the love is already there, waiting for activation. Your heart is where the love grows into the expression of your being. Activate it.

All the love you need is already in your own heart. Activate it.

**Emotions the author experienced:**

Love, resistance, confusion, individuality, sadness, despair, relief, optimism, hope, contentment.

## Love

*by Owen*

Love is the through line
The through line of love

Love.
A four-letter word
loaded like the barrel of a gun
deflated like a party balloon

Love
It lives in us
It comes for us

sometimes passes by us

Love
Heals and harms
has arms and legs
eyes and ears

Love
Has a swagger
and a sway
switching and twitching

Love
You feel it in your heart
You see it in another
You can't always receive it

Love
It's what we all long for
It lights our cells
And ignites our desires

Love
With or without you
For you and of you
Can it be you?
Love
Where are you?
I am blind
To you

Love
Do you taste?
Do you touch?
Do you smell?

Love
Too much
Too little
Too late

Love
I hate you
I need you
I want you

Love
Oh please
Love
Be kind...

Just Love.

LOVE


## Fill Up Your Love Cup

*by Holly*

Love is a resourceful state of being. Here's a guided meditation to help you find, activate, and connect to the love within you. When you crave love from others, you unknowingly give your power away, your ability to choose how you feel.

This is your permission slip, if you need it, to know that you deserve to be loved in exactly the way you desire. As Rumi said:

"*Your task is not to seek for love, but merely to seek and find all the barriers within yourself that you have built against it.*"

In other words, open yourself to letting love in, to loving your being, even though it can be vulnerable, terrifying, or even guilt- and shame-inducing. Let down the barriers to loving yourself first.

When it comes to others, you cannot control whether they love you. They must choose of their own free will. Their choice is a reflection of them, and not you.

**Visualization to Find, Activate, and Connect to Love**

Close your eyes and get comfortable, if you wish. Allow your attention to move inwards to your internal senses. Bring to your attention the experience of receiving love. Notice how it comes to you, any visuals, audio, smells, digestion movements, physical sensations, no matter how small, even the absence of them. Notice and thank them for coming to your awareness. Notice again.

Keep noticing and thanking until there are no more changes. Even a metaphor or idea may come through – go with whatever is there for you. You cannot get this wrong. What comes or resists for you is what you need to notice. It's exactly what's useful for you.

This is your representation of love, how your system experiences your love resource. Thank it for coming to your attention in this exact way. Invite your being to make any and all updates necessary for your love resource to be fully activated and most useful to you. Keep noticing and thanking. When you're ready, you can return your attention to what's present around you, knowing that the process will continue to continue.

Know that you can become present with the energy of receiving love whenever you need it. You can also use this process to give love to others and to activate any emotion you wish to work with.

*A recorded version of this meditation is available on the Courageous Hearts Collective website (courageous-hearts.com).*

# EMOTIONAL CHECK-IN

What emotions do you feel about the idea that love, like any emotion, is a choice?

When do you find it hardest to choose love, and what comes up for you in those moments?

What permission slip could you give yourself to explore love as a choice in your life?

# *Permission to give yourself what you needed when you were young*

## Sweaty Palms

*by Maggie*

Not enough ... says who?

Taking tests throughout my younger years in school, my sweat glands kicked into full force with the internal anxiety and nervousness that came from external pressure. I had no idea how to make logical sense of any of this. All I knew is that my hands sweated so much when I took a test in class, the paper was crinkled like parchment when I handed it in. All I knew was that my stomach churned and ached at school. All I knew was that this stomachache presented itself almost every morning before heading to school and that I responded as often as possible to stay home from school. The body knows anxiety and just reacts in a way to assist in releasing and comforting or balance.

My Little One did not know how to release anxiety by breathing to calm herself, by running away to what may seem like a "safe place," or screaming, or talking about how scared she was about questions on a piece of paper. All she knew was the nervous feeling in her stomach when the teacher handed out a test – watching as the test got closer to her desk and the nervousness was harder to handle. All my Little One knew was that the palms of her hands would flood with sweat even though she wiped them off on her skirt or pants. All she knew was that she didn't feel like she knew enough to pass a test perfectly, and that really scared her. All she knew was that it did not seem to be happening for the other kids around her, so she tried to hide, to blend in.

She did not know she had been "conditioned" by good parents to be a "good girl" who would perform according to someone else's standards. She did not know there was a part of her that began to develop in her psyche very early to cause her to question whether she was good enough. Who set the standards for "good"? That inner part would set her up for a lifetime of performance anxiety that internally would never give her an inch to be good enough. Instead, the pressure she felt had her body dripping with sweat onto her crinkled test paper that had even been reviewed for several extra minutes beyond completion to check and recheck every answer three or four times over. That was a lot of pressure for a Little One to handle! And she had no other perspective than to follow the rules that everyone else seemed to be following without question.

In the privacy at my desk during a test, my Little One struggled to hold the anxiety in check. My teachers never knew what I was dealing with, or if they did, they did not address it – perhaps they did not have the language or the know-how. The internal challenge of my "enoughness" was never discussed. My Little One did not like a grading scale on testing to confirm her enoughness, though that is all that the system was set up to rely upon.

My Little One longed for someone instead to be there for her with encouragement or a hand to hold when this anxiety washed over. The tender Little One, at an age of insecurity, knew nothing of an internal dialogue that nurtured and calmed an ever-strengthening part of me that was being groomed to perform with perfection.

I and my Little One knew nothing of a parent or teacher that would look me in the eye with full acceptance, love, and compassion to connect deep within me for assurance instead of holding up a measuring stick to compare me to others. Are you in the best reading group? Did your performance for the day get you to the front of the line to get to the restroom so you wouldn't pee your pants? Was your name on the chalkboard because you talked during class? Did you have to sit in the hall because your work was not done correctly, and then even more kids would see you weren't enough to be a good student? The fear and anxiety of the performance was monumental. Most days this tension was more than that Little One could face, and so the record-keeping of the report card had notes like, "Could do better," or comments from my mom that pushed me to go to school even if my stomachache had me in tears.

Years of this measuring pushed me through school, though at a major cost of actual learning or the chance to develop my love and connection with learning. The pressure to perform as a student was my most dedicated teacher – one with a critical eye that kept my raw, innocent voice from being accepted. My Brave Teenager was building an inner courage to yell a robust "Fuck You" under my breath at a teacher who cut me off when I was trying to formulate my words. The wound with the sharpness of inner criticism was quick and had the precision to penetrate into my body functions, whether it was sweaty palms, underarm circles on all my blouses, or the hesitation to raise my hand to speak that scared me away from thinking I mattered for most of my years in school. A teenager wants so deeply to be accepted, and my inner teenager felt more and more like an outcast.

Do you know these parts of me are still alive and well, though buried deep within me? I've learned to be a good performer. My body still lets me know when something or someone triggers feelings of anxiety to perform perfectly. The sweat glands offer their signals, even though the initial "performance" or anxious event happened decades ago. The wounds run deep and get buried. The body can even show up with physical malperformance, like viral symptoms. That's the power of the energy of emotions.

As I reflect on the experiences of these parts that still exist within my grown-up body, I can have a more mature and experienced perspective. But the wounds are not something that can be dealt with on a logical level; they are the emotions of parts of me that have been frozen at their time of maturity and are still calling out for love and acceptance at the point where they are stuck. The journey is to take my present-day self back to their side to support, love, and accept them, just as they are – releasing all judgment, as that powerful force has kept these parts separated like outcasts.

I would invite you to imagine some parts of yourself at an early age that did not get the attention and love they wanted. Just notice them in your mind's eye. Whether you know it or not, they have influenced you throughout your lifetime. They may feel resistant because they have been neglected and judged for a long time (by you and by others, though it's you that can attend to them). Just hold this experience of connecting with them for a moment – nothing needs to be said, and nothing needs to be done. You are holding a space of awareness that allows you to see them and them to see you. Perhaps you are noticing a slight release of tension in your body. If not, that's OK. To be with a younger part of yourself for just a minute is a beautiful gift, because the moment back in time when this developing self did not have someone to comfort or hold them is an opportunity you can now address.

So many times, we look outside ourselves to be acknowledged or told we are good enough. What I am noticing now is that I have the tools through a moment of awareness to comfort my Little One in a way that no one else knows how to do. I have the tools to give my Brave Teen an imaginary high-five when she wants to shout out a "fuck you" in her room, when she and I feel like we are not seen or heard. That frustration is real and lives in us as emotional build-up. The body holds this.

These parts of us are a normal development in our psychology and a healthy pattern for growing up. They are well researched and have been shared with understanding through such work as Voice Dialogue by Hal and Sidra Stone, both PhD.

**Emotions the author experienced:**

Anxiety, doubt, meaninglessness, compassion.

## Responding to Maggie

*by Owen*

Dear Sweaty Palms,

You are a magnificent truth teller, and so brave.

I see you and feel you and have my own version of sweaty palms. Mine lives in my throat and chest, with a tightening grip that retreats into silence, with a heat that shows up at the back of my neck and then I sweat. I'm not sure I would have been able to speak and own my version of sweaty palms if you hadn't graced the pages of Maggie's writing. Thank you for coming forward to share your vulnerability and impeccable intel.

My guess is that we all have a version of sweaty palms that longs to be witnessed and loved for all of her gifts. Her gift of knowing that something just isn't right for her, the gift of our bodies' wisdom telling us to pay attention, the gift that we get to heal this place in ourselves so we can choose differently. So, reader, what is your "Sweaty Palm" story? Is it a body sensation? Or perhaps a sound? Do you know what triggers her? Take a moment to check in with yourself and see if you can get a glimpse, and then offer her some compassion and love. She is a doorway to healing a younger part.

Deep gratitude and love,

Owen

# EMOTIONAL CHECK-IN

What emotions do you feel about meeting the unmet needs of your younger self?

What is your version of 'Sweaty Palms'? How does it show up in your life, and what does it reveal about your younger self's needs?

What permission slip could you give yourself to better meet the needs of that younger part of you?

# Permission to not know

## Mercy, Mercy, Mercy
*by Deborah*

Another January, facing another blank sheet as we gather to prime the pumps (or reboot them) for our book.

I'm tempted to say I'm a blank slate with nothing to offer, but that would be a lie. I know I have something to offer, but right now it's buried beneath a pile of uncomfortable thoughts and feelings.

I'm awash in sadness that is out of sync with the beautiful, sunny day and my cozy surroundings. This week I've been missing my girl like crazy. My heart aches. I long to embrace her, inhale the ripe, earthy odor that I teased her about so many times. No amount of gratitude, joy, or delight in the present moment has what it takes to ease the pain.

My body remembers the lumbering heaviness of late pregnancy, 30 years ago – a stark contrast to the sorrow that fills me now.

To create a container for our writing, Maggie pulls an oracle card: Quan Yin, Mother of Mercy. Ah, yes. Mercy. Compassion. Forgiveness. I sure could use some of that now. Mercy for things said and unsaid, done and undone. Compassion for still being mired in grief, longing for what can never be.

Tears flow. Snot runs. Heart aches. Head throbs. Arms long to hold and be held.

Fear and doubt creep in. What will it take to be fully present to life again? To embrace the moment, not as a temporary escape from the empty sadness/sad emptiness, but to truly experience the fullness of what is, in exquisite detail.

I feel caught in that old tug of war between Too Much and Not Enough, as I navigate a budding relationship. Too much sadness and pain, and not enough trust. Do I trust him to embrace the grieving mother as warmly as the sparkly, sassy woman? Do I trust myself enough to reveal her?

Mercy, mercy, mercy ...

The voice of Not Enough has been loud these days. Not creative enough. Not wise enough. Not enough that's worth saying. Not inspiring enough. Trite. Shallow. Inconsequential. Have mercy on those who have to read my drivel...

As I spew this bile, the tension in my head and shoulders loosens its grip. The tears and snot let up. My head is still devoid of inspiration, but it's no longer berating me. A lull in the onslaught. Perhaps that's what mercy looks like in this moment in time.

What is Mercy's invitation for me? *Pause. Breathe. Listen.*

A bell from a nearby church. A plane overhead. The tinnitus crickets that are my constant companions. Traffic. My breath. Feet scuffling the floor under my chair.

There are plenty of sounds to fill my ears when I let go of listening to the stale, negative thoughts that I was supposed to set aside for this retreat.

Still no sign of inspiring thoughts, but I'm okay with that in this moment. Sometimes small mercies are enough.

Embrace the dial tone (or, in my case, the crickets). Let it be enough. No, let it be just right.

Listen to the urge to curl up for a while. The page is no longer blank. Trust that more will come, in due time.

**Emotions the author experienced:**

Sadness, grief, compassion, fear, doubt, trust.

# EMOTIONAL CHECK-IN

What emotions does "not knowing" or "not having all the answers" stir up for you?

How does the feeling of "not knowing" show up in your life, and what do you typically do when it arises?

What permission slip could you give yourself to relax into not knowing, without needing to fix or solve it for a moment?

# Permission to choose

## Responsibility

*by Holly*

Responsibility – Response and Ability with "I" in the middle.

Between stimulus and response is I. I am the one who notices the experiences of my life.

With a little attention, you can notice any stimulus and develop the ability to respond from I, rather than from automated reactions.

Reactions – re-actions – repeating actions of the past.

I can be still and know. Know what I want. Know which way to go. Know what is happening for others swept up in the sea of emotion-based thinking. Know how to respond to the events of life as I experience them. This is the sea of tranquility.

The ocean in which it seems as if you are drowning is really the layers of stuck emotion and old beliefs that are calling for your attention. Calling you to take responsibility to resolve, update, relax, and heal. Breaking the bond of inherited sin, of intergenerational trauma, and instead learning how to make your choices truly your own. Discovering how to stop reacting and start responding from a resourceful state of being.

Sin is commonly thought of as doing or being wrong. This is a false teaching. To sin means to go against one's own divine being, to ignore your knowing, whether by conscious or unconscious choice. For most of us, it's unconscious. As the stimulus occurs, the reaction happens, and I am not part of the decision nor able to make a true response.

This is an incredible survival mechanism when you really think about it. Put your hand on a hot stove, and the fact that the unconscious reaction is to pull it off without thinking is incredible. When it comes to truly thriving in life, not just surviving, I need to be able to bring my attention to the tiny space after a stimulus, so that I can be present and choose my response.

Let go of carrying responsibility for what's not yours. You are too open to others' emotions and needs because you don't want them to experience what you experienced. On some level, you are still judging what happened to you as good or bad, saintly or sinful. Things happen without a why. It's not your fault. It's not because you are not enough, or bad, or not competent. What elders don't heal, we, especially as children, carry for them. We inherit the sins of the forefathers and foremothers as we then take on responsibility for healing within ourselves, what they did not.

Seek the lessons and gifts in your suffering – they are the way home to your true being. When we see the gifts of our wounding, release self-blame, self-shame and self-judgment, then we see we never needed to be saved. Rather than trying to save others, you can show them the way back to their true self and natural expression, just as you are finding the way back to connection with your own being right now.

As a child, I became incredibly sensitive and empathic. It was a gift I developed out of necessity to keep myself safe in a chaotic household. I took on responsibilities that were not mine to resolve. It was a way that I gained attention, love, and safety. Predicting my mother's needs, reading her mood, anticipating her thoughts helped me care for myself. If I could make her life easier, then mine was better. My life as a little one was dependent on her, my joy or pain on her state.

I learned that to care for myself I needed to be responsible for the woman on whom my life depended. I learned that to stay safe I could not reveal my true self to her. I learned that my emotions and needs were less important, wrong, or selfish, or to be hidden. I made her emotions and thoughts the highest priority in order to stay safe. I was unable to be myself. All of my gifts were channeled into managing my mother. I say this not out of resentment, simply to share a profound realization resulting from my personal experiences.

What our elders don't take responsibility for, we the children carry for them. Sometimes the elders have their own unhealed wounds and suffer greatly. Their pain is like a hot potato, a flaming red ball that has been passed on to us. You hold it for them, falsely believing you must have done something to deserve this, that there must be a reason why you feel this intense pain. It's not your fault, dear one, it's the unhealed wounds of others. No wonder so many of us don't want to face our pain and suffering, opting instead to avoid what we don't want to experience again.

Who in their right mind would want to go into an emotional space that they haven't been given the resources to handle? Who would want to catch that hot potato without some heat-proof gloves and the ability to cool it down and handle it safely? Our ancestors inadvertently throw us the hot potatoes that they couldn't handle. Sometimes we simply need to stop being there to catch the hot potato. It's like a bad habit that stops us playing the game of life.

Getting emotionally resourceful changes the game. It opens up the space to not only survive, but thrive in the joy of responsible living, regardless of how challenging the environment outside may be. Responsibility should not feel heavy; it is supposed to feel balanced and harmonious, like a light cool breeze in the sunshine. If it feels like a weight dragging you down, restricting your breath, then you may be taking on too much responsibility or even avoiding some.

### Emotions the author experienced:

Self-authority, passion, well-being, hope, optimism, contentment, awe.

## Claiming My Voice

*by Owen*

The power to claim my voice is my responsibility. This lands like a thud in my gut.

When we are young, we look to our elders to light the way, mirror for us how to nurture and be nurtured. Somewhere along the way, we lose our most natural authentic voice. I know I have lost and found mine throughout my life. But it has felt like a slippery penny in my pocket, and my ability to avoid conflict and be the peacekeeper at all costs has muted my voice. I have kept quiet.

I am a combination of a highly sensitive introvert with an extrovert side kick. Which means I like my own company and enjoy the company of others and have to gear up for large gatherings and need recovery time after. I love the energy of large crowds, concerts, cities, and then I need to recover. It's a balance. My voice moves with me. Together, we are learning to stretch and include writing as part of my repertoire. I am a visual artist, and my voice is comfortable creating with color, pattern, and texture. But words have also felt daunting, less mysterious, too black and white.

The last two years, writing for and with this collaborative book, have given voice to things I might not have dared say on the page. I have heard from astrologers, my Akashic Records teacher, and practice partners that my voice wants to be heard. My voice wants a bigger stage. This is terrifying to me, and exciting. My introvert could be OK leaving the words on the page and skipping along. But this part of me that's stage-bound, extroverted, perhaps also a rebel, is tired of being told to rest on the side lines. She wants to try out some new places to be heard. A call to the wild, of sorts! I wonder what this will look like.

A little back story of my voice: I was diagnosed with thyroid cancer 20+ years ago and was in remission. Being checked every 6 months and with annual ultrasounds, I was OK. Then in early 2022, two cancerous nodules were found on the right side of my neck where my cancerous thyroid used to be. "Ants at a picnic," my doctor said – implying there were probably more. He was right.

As my cancer does not respond to traditional radioactive iodine, I elected for a neck dissection.

The beautiful Dr. Glenda (I think of her as my good witch) operated and took out seven lymph nodes, and five were cancerous. A shock and a relief. I continue to live with cancer and don't know what's next, but should it continue to grow more, I face more surgery. So it's not a coincidence that the cancer and the surgery are in my neck, the space of my voice. The voice I have so beautifully curated to accommodate, control, stay quiet, keep the peace, speak with loving kindness, stay safe – and by all means, don't let the rebel speak, for she will clear the room! At the times when she has boiled over and cleared the room, it's exhilarating, exhausting, toxic, truth-telling, and messy. But this rebel has a voice that wants to play, dream, live more, love more, and experience the mess from a place of love, self-love. As I feel into her and listen, I notice that her voice has changed.

Two surgeries to my neck have created scar tissue and some numbness; my voice has changed. Singing feels and sounds different, people have commented that my voice sounds different. It is. This rebel voice is tender, scarred, scared, and ready to take her place on the stage of my life.

As I write this, a warmth has come across my body, a knowing, a whisper, and an invitation to step out, be heard, be seen, and be received. Ahh, there it is! The infinite loop of giving, showing up, and receiving. To be received, one needs to shine, be seen and heard.

This emerging space of my voice has a message for me: Don't waste any more time waiting for the time to be right. The right time is already here.

Just getting this out on paper feels right! The black and white words putting a mark on the page. A call for more!

What does "more" look like? Feel like? In my body and my heart? What are the sounds that want to come out? Is there a color or texture to this space of more? I know that like anything I have ever embraced, it's really putting one foot in front of the other and a daily practice of trusting that I don't know what the new "more" is, but am willing to listen, experience.

And shine.

I also have this incredible group of collaborators in writing to share, try things on, and hold the space of this new voice. My new/old voice. The fully actualized voice that is embracing my introvert with so much loving kindness, sharing the stage with her. We step out and speak, dance, breathe, laugh, cry, and yell at the top of our lungs, "I GET TO LIVE," "I AM LIVING WITH CANCER," "CANCER LIVES WITH ME".... WHAT THE FUCK!!!

Yup, it's a FUCKED kind of paradox! But then, isn't life funny that way? Full of paradoxes. Some black and white, and some with a lot of gray but nonetheless paradoxes. That's right, get comfortable with the uncomfortable, for that is truly the gift of being alive and awake.

I am grateful every day that I have cancer that isn't going to kill me. I am lucky. I have accepted this and now share it more openly when people ask about my cancer. There is often a pregnant pause, for the idea of living with cancer seems radical, foreign, uncomfortable, unknown.

For me, it is a gift of the most imperfect perfect life I get to live. I think of my cancer as my friend, my rebel with a cause. She has a voice and will no longer live in the shadows. She shines like a penny and has many thoughts to express. Recently I have wondered about the healing that will come from allowing this "more" voice to live? My guess is there is a possible miracle to be had. As I continue to raise my resonance and my voice, will it cure my cancer?

A little bit of miracle magic to sprinkle along the way. Who knows? What I do know is sharing my words in black and white, speaking them and experiencing them as we raise the volume, is healing. A journey to become more whole.

### Emotions the author experienced:

Fear, abandonment, anger, love, self-authority, compassion, well-being.

## Today I Showed Up for Myself
*by Marna*

Today I showed up for myself.
I rolled out my yoga mat and began *Day 1 with Adrienne*.
It doesn't sound like much, doing some yoga.
After all, lots of people do yoga every day.

But for me, it was huge.
I had forgotten yoga.
I had forgotten my body.

Is "forgotten" the right word, though?
It's really quite hard to forget.

No, I had ignored my body.
Dismissed it, minimized it.
Tried to silence it.

My body will not be silenced.

My body is my alarm system,
doing its job to tell me something's wrong.
It jolts me awake at night, again and again,
trying to tell me to
Pay attention!

It wakes me up with panic,
Then it moves on to outrage.

Every night my body has been screaming:
*Pay attention to me!*
*Why won't you just pay attention to me?*
*What more do I have to do*
*to get you to notice me and to say I matter!?!?*

It's speaking up for me.
It's taking a stand for my life and legacy.

At night, I feel the panic as I consider my human fragility and mortality.
Then remorse, shame, and despair roll in for what I've done to it.
I feel the outrage and anger as I mentally put my foot down:
Enough is enough!
I vow to make it right.
Tomorrow.

In the light of day, often,
the exhaustion and self-pity and shame
weigh me down like a blanket.

The pull of comfort – or at least, the familiar "autopilot" route – is strong and compelling.
I distract myself from the incredible discomfort of being in my own skin by being busy.

I console myself for the places I fail to show up in the way I know I could
by stuffing down the frustration, self-blame, and shame
with gourmet coffee and baked goods.
I deserve this treat, I tell myself sympathetically,
after the morning I've had.
Self-medication, soothing, burying the shame so I don't have to feel it anymore.
Buried under pounds of flesh.
And that caged animal feeling.

I'm putting myself in that cage.

So, it matters that today, I showed up for myself!
Today I made a promise to myself – to my body – that I would do yoga when I got home.
I'd already dressed in comfortable clothes and everything.

I sat on the mat, ready. Poised.

As I began the practice, the fact that I had showed up for myself in such a
powerful and life-giving way sank in,
and I felt a homecoming, as my body said, Thank You!
*Thank you for listening!*
And this deep gratitude and relief gave way to grief,
and I started sobbing, releasing the heartbreak as I finally felt what had
been lost all these years.
I was finally here in my body,
I'd come to it via yoga, which always felt like home for me.

A remembering,
though I'd never forgotten it.
Rather, a re-membering, as I put a big, sacred piece of myself back together.

And when all the tears were shed,
My whole body sighed in relief.
Yes. YES.

I turned my attention to the practice,
reintroducing the places in my body that were reluctant,
slowly and steadily easing in.

As the practice came to a close,
I lay on my back, palms together, whispering,
"Thank you, thank you, thank you,"
to my body, my Inner Child, my Higher Self, the universe, everyone.
We all said thank you to one another.
Thank you for being here.

It's moments like these that shape my journey.
Because, truly, This Moment, now, is all I ever have to make a difference.

So, I can decide to show up for myself.

Then, I choose again.
Then, I take action.
Then, I celebrate.
Then, I store it away to remember.

For when I am faced with another fork in the road,
I can call upon this moment again.
Be inspired again, to decide.
Be resolved again, to choose.
Be willing again, to act.

Every step forward I choose to take for the sake of myself creates a feedback loop.
It feeds me the love I need to take another step forward:
I've done this before.
I can do it again.
I remember how amazing it felt.
I know I am worth it.

Each time I choose to create a space in my day
to do something just for me and no one else
 – just because I WANT TO –
is a huge triumph!

It's me putting a stake in the ground: I Matter.

One step at a time.
One moment at a time.
One choice at a time.
I am forging a path of Love towards
greater
Individuality,
Joy,
Self-authority
and Freedom.

YES!

**Emotions the author experienced:**

Panic, remorse, shame, despair, outrage, anger, grief, love, joy, freedom, self-authority, happiness, well-being.

# EMOTIONAL CHECK-IN

What emotions arise when you think about taking responsibility for the life you are creating?

Where in your life could you take more responsibility, or hand back responsibility that's not yours to carry?

What permission slip could you give yourself to fully claim responsibility for your choices and way forward?

# Permission to claim self-authority

## The Path from Anger to Self-Authority

by Marna

These past few weeks, I've been fighting a growing urge to retreat into hiding. That familiar tape playing in my mind – the one telling me I'm not good enough – has gotten louder and more broad-sweeping. It says I don't deserve to be in this group, to be a coach, to have a business, to be parenting my children, you name it. Why? Because I'm not evolved enough. My voice and experience don't matter. I'm not reliable. I'm screwing everything up. I'm disappointing everyone. I don't have what it takes. I'm a failure.

It's heartbreaking to hear these condemning words in my head again as I write this. I can feel anguish rise up – it's a younger part of myself crying out. I've been sensing her there over these past weeks, feeling her heart breaking as she listens to this onslaught of judgments. When I've given her space to express her heartbreak, I find myself overcome by body-heaving sobs.

And yet, amidst that suffering, beneath the despair and hopelessness, I'd begun to notice stirrings of some other emotion. When I was finally able to get still and connect to it, I heard a teenaged part of myself cry out in protest: *It's not fair! Why do you say these things?!*

The emotion was anger. It was telling me a line has been crossed.

Over the days that follow, I sit with this teenaged part of me often, to hear what she else has to say: *Why are you putting all this pressure on me? I'm trying my best here! FUCK!!!! What do you want from me!??!?*

It's not just anger. It's rage. Rage at being dismissed and criticized, told she's not enough, and made to feel she doesn't matter, over and over and over again.

She's furious: *How dare you speak to me this way again and again!? How dare you treat me this way! It's mean! You're so mean!*

She's right. What I've been longing for, more than anything, is to experience enduring self-compassion, love, and acceptance … but how can I hope to when the narration of unworthiness is so loud and ever-present?

I learned a while ago that the voice of unworthiness is my Inner Critic – the judging voice I've internalized from a society attempting to keep me safe, protected, and controlled. I know that it can be helpful to create distance from it, to stop identifying with it.

But it's hard to do this when it keeps masquerading as "my" voice, using "facts" from my past to prove I don't measure up. I keep being convinced of its authority.

And yet, my Inner Teen is showing me a reliable way of separating myself from it: by allowing in my anger, feeling it fully, and hearing what it wants to say.

Anger shows up when things aren't fair. When a boundary has been crossed. When our needs are not being met. Anger fuels the courage to speak up for ourselves when we're being treated unjustly.

When we dismiss Anger's voice again and again, it turns into Rage, which helps us take a stand for our dignity, our mattering.

Giving voice to my anger and rage gives me access to MY voice. Listening to my anger and rage, I'm hearing a boundary being created between my Inner Critic's damaging self-talk and the rest of me.

I have a right to be angry! I have a right to be enraged! I would NEVER allow someone I love to be spoken to or treated in this way. I can feel the impact of allowing my Inner Teen space to FEEL. She feels validated and encouraged to keep speaking up, speaking out, speaking her truth.

I feel myself using the energy of this anger to put my foot down against this harmful inner self-talk. I feel myself taking a stand for being treated with dignity, respect, kindness, and love.

And I feel a larger truth waiting for me to grab hold of:

My BEING is ENOUGH.

My PRESENCE is ENOUGH!

I Matter, just by BEING!

In creating a boundary between these damaging lies of unworthiness and the rest of me, I can FEEL myself walking the path to claim my self-authority.

This is what my path to self-authority looks like:

It's choosing, moment by moment,
To recognize the lies of unworthiness,
To resist the illusion of familiarity
and the pull to shrink and stay small.

It's choosing instead to feel the pain,
to listen to the anger in protest.
To stand my ground
and put the boundaries in place.

And, it's choosing to have the courage
to give myself what I want and need.

**Emotions the author experienced:**

Worthlessness, despair, hopelessness, anger, rage, self-authority, hurt.

# EMOTIONAL CHECK-IN

What emotions do you feel in relation to claiming your self-authority and giving yourself what you need and want?

In what areas of your life do you struggle to claim what you need or want, and why?

What permission slip could support you in expanding the courage to give yourself what you need and want?

# Permission to show yourself grace and compassion

## Covid Loneliness
*by Owen*

I am on the mat. I haven't been here since before the pandemic; my body is excited and a little shy. As I breathe into the postures the yoga teacher is gently guiding us through between long intentional breaths, I begin to notice the grief that is knotted into my shoulders like rocks sunk into the sand at the beach. The mat seems to be bringing in the tide, a rhythm to move these knots of grief and allow them to move out. I notice the ache in my body from not being in an in-person yoga class for over 3 years ... an ache for connection, community and movement that sings to my soul. My mat. The rocks of grief need not be analyzed or figured out; they are the clusters and collections over time lodged in my body. I continue to move through poses I haven't held in a long time; my breath and my mat keep me grounded and present. I find myself asking, "What is really present here now?"

A sensation rolls through my body with a singular tone, a vibration that feels at once old and recent. The emotion of loneliness resonates and breathes through me. My chest tightens and my heart aches ... the knowing of this dark place of loneliness. My mat continues to hold me, grounding me in the present. This loneliness is sitting alone on her mat, grateful for the mat, a place to be and breathe. The class ends and I am grateful for the awareness and feel myself wanting to run from loneliness. Oh no, not you!

My loneliness is a loaded gun pointed at my psyche. Alone in a dark room, in a hard chair, unable to see or find the light. The week progresses and I am being followed and called to this place of loneliness. It's now hanging heavy in my chest and heart like a lead balloon, choking my breath, clouding my vision and gripping my voice. Tears sit just below the surface.

I spend the next few days trying to outrun loneliness as overwhelm and panic roll in, vibrating through my core. There is no hiding, running or compartmentalizing this loneliness anymore – it needs to be expressed. I feel into this loneliness and begin to feel it move slowly, revealing its tenderness and vulnerability. Tears flow. I find an opportunity presents itself to share this loneliness with my partner and what I'm noticing about being on my mat in a yoga class.

This recognition of my emotions and asking to be witnessed releases another layer of loneliness. The panic and overwhelm dissolve as a connection is made and my breath lengthens.

A few days later, I am back on my mat in a yoga class. I am loneliness. She and I are not alone in this place, but together and exploring. The exploration starts with asking, "Who is lonely? What part of me? How old am I?" I can see and feel all the parts of myself step forward to announce themselves like a roll call. Oddly, this loneliness has a new edge, flavor, and rhythm…

I continue through the poses, breathing, stretching, releasing, and easing into my body, becoming more fluid. The fluidity allows me to notice the sensations, aches, and whispers of this loneliness. It's what I call the Covid Loneliness. She was born in Covid and has a global experience. She feels big. My mat is feeling crowded with this loneliness. Is there enough room for us here on the mat? A relief rolls in when class is brought to an end.

Loneliness and I co-exist in the coming days, living together uncomfortably, aware that we have a friend in grief and sadness. We have tossed out our fishing line in the hopes of connection and love. The line sits slack in the waters of uncertainty, waiting for a bite or a tug. The reminder that I/we are not alone in our shared loneliness. The Covid Loneliness is a double-edged sword. It brings connection through a shared distanced global experience over the airways – a nice way of seemingly sharing the weight of loneliness. Yet for me, there is no comfort in knowing there has been a global experience of Covid Loneliness. This just adds another rock to my pile of grief and a physical separation that has eroded the world I used to know. The loneliness I knew so well and visited sometimes has new weight, not just in my shoulders, but in my heart and chest.

Do you feel this too, reader? Covid Loneliness? How does it show up in your body?

Have you identified the voice of loneliness? Have you found your way to the mat? What are the ways you are moving through to find love and connection?

I step back on my mat again, and this time the class size has grown to capacity. I feel the breath, not just to my mat but to the others in the room. We begin to breathe and move together at our own pace, stopping long enough to feel the connection before moving to the next pose. I feel my chest, heart, shoulders begin to ease and relax and receive this class with gratitude and grace. I am at once alone on my mat and in the community practicing yoga. I feel the grip of Covid Loneliness begin to dissolve as my jaw softens and I smile at others in the room. This re-entry to the world with the lag of loneliness is clunky and awkward, and with it comes so much possibility of hope, love, and connection.

Oh, the beautiful faces of Covid Loneliness. Together we will continue to move through with our breath and gratitude, knowing that just for this moment we can choose to be together again in person. It feels so good to be in person again intentionally. Let us not forget, but choose to connect.

### Emotions the author experienced:

Loneliness, grief, overwhelm, panic, freedom, self- authority, hope, love.

# EMOTIONAL CHECK-IN

What emotions have you experienced in the last 24-48 hours?

Are any of these emotions still present for you now?

What permission slip could help you slow down, connect with your emotions, and show yourself more grace and self-compassion?

# *Permission to trust the sacred*

**A Letter from My Soul**

*by Deborah*

Maggie pulls a card as a writing prompt: *"Say what your Soul needs to say."*

As I sit quietly and reflect on this invitation, the whispers emerge and I capture what I hear:

> *I have so much love and compassion for you, dear woman. You were thrown into unthinkable turbulence without a moment's notice and found a way to navigate that reality in the midst of your anguish. And you held fast to what would keep you on course: your abiding love for your girl, and your fierce commitment to honor her spirit.*
>
> *The depth of your pain and sorrow is a testament to your willingness to accept and to feel. Some call it courage – to step into the fray with your heart fully present, whatever may happen. That takes love, and trust, and fierce commitment – to yourself, and to your belief in the power and value of experiencing your emotions, come what may.*
>
> *You're uncomfortable when people admire your courage. "I'm not brave, I'm just willing," you reply. The invitation is for you to be willing to see yourself as courageous, to tap into that courage and*

*dare to have a voice that matters, that moves others to find their willingness, their courage.*

*You are a beacon to those who fear they may be overwhelmed by their emotions or dashed to pieces on the rocks, if they dare to let themselves feel them. You have weathered the storm, time and time again, and lived to tell the tale. That's no small thing. Don't minimize it.*

*You are an anchor for those who fear they will be swept away.*

*You are a harbor for those who seek shelter. A hearth for those who need a warm place to call home.*

*You are the Goddess for those who are not afraid of their own divinity and who can come into her presence with humility, gratitude, and delight.*

*You don't have to try to be those things. It's your nature. You can't help it, and you can't hide it. Folks are gonna see it anyway. You might as well own it. Grace the world with it, for as long as you are here. (HAVE YOU LEARNED NOTHING FROM YOUR LOSS???)*

*Shit's about to get real. (Shhh! It's about to get real!) Indeed, it is already happening. Don't hide behind your grief. Feel it, yes, but use it to fuel your compassion, with mercy and love.*

*Your heart is a vessel overflowing with love. Share it, sing it, be it. Above all, don't hide it.*

Was this message from my Soul? My Higher Self? My subconscious?

Does it matter who it's from???

No! What matters is the message and the powerful permission slips it conveyed.

Permission to embrace courage. Permission to own my power. Permission to recognize the gifts of my grief.

Permission to trust the sacred.

Emotions the author experienced:

Love, compassion, curiosity, trust, self-authority, courage.

# Facing the Darkness

*by Maggie*

My dad died twenty-three years ago. It could have happened yesterday, as my mind vividly remembers every moment. Do you have moments in your life that slow down, preserving every detail? I had gone on a trip to California and Vancouver when my dad began his journey to the end of life. I remember the last words he said to me: "You go and have a good time." I had a fleeting thought that he was taking a turn for the worse, since he was getting weaker, though my mind preferred the comfort of denial.

In California, I stayed with a long-time friend and coach who offered me support by sharing with me her copy of *The Tibetan Book of Living and Dying*. She was more in touch with the possibility of my dad's transition than I was at the time. She knew I was still in denial. I opened the book to read how to accept death and to support the journey of dying. I thought my friend had offered this book to read for my dad. It soon became clear this book was for me – to prepare for his transition – and, as his only daughter, that I too would go through a sort of death – my final role as his daughter. I recognized that we were preparing to face our transitions together and acknowledged the profound experience that lay ahead for us. I wanted to be a courageous presence for him, like he had been for me on so many occasions.

Several days passed, and I stayed in touch with my brothers who were at the hospital, keeping me updated on Dad's condition. He was stable except for some breathing complications that the doctors were able to quickly address. The day I boarded the plane home I'd heard that hospice had been called. What I thought would be a part business, part pleasure trip out West had quickly morphed into a crash course for me to find the courage I needed to be with my dad during his death.

The trip was exhausting and emotionally draining. I headed home from the airport to rest, as I would be taking the 4 am shift to be at Dad's bedside to relieve my brother and sister-in-law and give them some much-needed respite. When I arrived at the hospital, I found my sweet dad hooked up to tubes, in a brightly lit room with a blaring TV. Whether because I was still tired from my trip or due to some inner nudge for attending the soul's transition – whatever the reason, I knew that the room needed to be cleared so that I could bring in loving comfort for my dad. Lights out, TV off, door closed to mute the conversations from the nurse's station – outside intrusions were reduced. We had a journey to take.

I sat in the darkness looking at my dad. I cried. I spoke softly of how much I loved him. I could sense he was already a few steps ahead of me. I felt too far away sitting in a chair and was still a bit tired from my trip, so I thought I would lay down beside him in his hospital bed. I could then hear his breathing while feeling the comfort of knowing I was exactly where I needed to be.

I didn't think I would fall asleep, so I was surprised when I got a tap on my left shoulder. I expected it was a nurse waking me up to scoot me out of the bed. It was still dark. I looked around; no one was there. I heard silence – no TV, no nurses, and no breathing. I didn't want to move. I could sense the darkness as a comfort. I could feel the sacredness of his soul still present. I will never forget that feeling. Time stood still, and I may have stopped breathing, too, as I lay there in awe, touching the sacred moment of his transition. My dad waited for me to journey him across. And as if to jolt away the darkness, the sun burst its first beam into the hospital room, declaring it was 7 am on All Saint's Day. My dear dad had moved on, and it still feels like it happened only yesterday.

*Let the dark times season you.*

*~ Hafiz*

### Emotions the author experienced:

Feeling hollow, sadness, love.

# EMOTIONAL CHECK-IN

What emotions do you feel about trusting the sacred?

What does "the sacred" mean to you, and how do you experience it in your life?

Is there a permission slip you could give yourself to lean into the sacred, even in times of challenge or grief?

# Permission to heal

## Patterns Stuck Within Us

*by Maggie*

Our bodies can store our emotional stories (or patterns), physically and energetically. We are probably aware of this, especially an inner knowing of body sensations. Consider what you may feel or sense when you speak of something that happened to you years ago that still gets repeated (indicates a stuck pattern), or how you may become agitated emotionally when someone else has a story that "triggers" a response within you (like a remembering or something that goes against a personal belief), or perhaps when you feel a certain body sensation within you when you remember a certain event in your life (also a sign of a stuck pattern).

Our physical bodies and beyond are tuned in to those patterns that vibrate outside our visible awareness. Have you ever stepped into a room after an argument, where you could feel the emotional energy, or after a celebration of a new grandchild? Another example of a stuck emotional pattern for me is when the weather changes to fall. I can still have a perceived stomachache that is reminiscent of the anxiety I felt as a young person when shifting from my free days of summer, a reminder of feeling trapped at school with rules, performance, and regulations that my younger self did not like to conform to.

We may think we move on from these stories, though most of us still can feel stuck with little to no awareness that the emotional patterns are actually at the root. We've been trained to not think about our emotions, so we think we are numb to them. The BIG NEWS, though, is that they are stuck within us. While you may not have much awareness, the pattern is still within your operating system.

How do we incorporate and welcome this valuable part of ourselves? The first step is to become aware, and the body is very good at offering messages for that awareness. Some body sensations could be in the form of headaches, overthinking that drains our energy, busy-ness that keeps us distracted, shame and guilt that keep us from our greatness, thyroid issues, hip and knee pain – the list of physical sensations and conditions that are rooted in an emotional and thought patterning goes on and on.

An emerging practice called Biofield Tuning offers a way to notice (beyond thinking) these energetic patterns of emotions and stories vibrationally while "combing" a person's energetic field using well-defined tuning forks. This work has been pioneered by Eileen McKusick in her documented research, practical applications, and studies for over 25 years. She has even proposed a mapped patterning of emotions to certain areas of a person's body where those emotions are commonly held energetically and vibrationally. Our emotions, she proposes, are of magnetic charge (also associated with the feminine), and our thoughts work on electricity (associated with the masculine). In our physical form, we are electromagnetic beings, combining masculine and feminine to work together. Like a working battery, both the positive (masculine) and the negative (feminine) charges must be active to ignite the voltage.

Our bodies need that balance, too. For centuries, our culture has been steeped in the drive of the mind and the intellect (masculine patriarchy) that has tilted our human being-ness into heavy, overloaded doing-ness. As a result of years of denial and sometimes fear of our emotions (feminine), the human body has absorbed this imbalance, filling us with unprecedented levels of stress, both physical and mental. With this imbalance we have lost sight and sensation of our natural connection to our emotions.

What is being called forward now is the balance of the magnetic and the electrical pulses of life to bring us into a voltage of light and energy. This major shift is available to everyone! We are being called to feel our emotions – initially by, through, and with full awareness of them, feeling and flowing with the full range gifted to us as humans.

The gift of the book you are holding is more and more awareness and appreciation to recognize, connect, and feel our emotions. Let's let our natural light shine!

## Claiming Our Magnificence

*by Holly*

I take a deep breath. I feel overwhelmed writing more. *Isn't it enough yet?*, moans my inner teenager. Meanwhile, my 5-year-old self is playing on her typewriter in the attic saying, *I want to do this all day!* I, at this moment, am sore in a weighty body that's clinging on to old patterns of reaction, rather than responsibility. Slow to claim my authority, visibility, magnificence.

Are we all feeling this way? Afraid to be with our magnificence? It's so easy to fall for the illusion that we are powerless victims in this world, or grappling for our power, earning it, proving we deserve to claim it by overcoming the "not us" and the masks we've learned to wear. And yet, when we accept all of what we feel, we see we are a multicolored mess – a kaleidoscope of all the shades of the rainbow.

I am not this black and white, good or bad, right or wrong model of the universe. I am all of that, and so much more. I am vibrant, multicolored magnificence. In the past, I would have felt guilt and shame for claiming that. I would never have let it all hang out on show. Being visible and heard was scary, terrifying in fact. But that was my story of being a helpless victim.

Owen suggested that I am already living my great life story, and I chose to claim that. To accept it, with a big, exciting, and scary ah-ha moment. My magnificence is already unfolding in its own awkward, different, shining out, bright and loud, weird, and sometimes quiet and still way. I am all of it. One day one way, the next another – a dynamic, shifting sense of self that can't be boxed up or held to a snapshot sliver of my identity.

What is identity, anyway? It's what we identify with. The stories, the emotions, the thoughts, the meanings, the sense of self we claim as "me." What if I dropped all that static? What if I said, "No more," to having my future defined by what I did and who I was yesterday. Today is a new day. I get to make new choices. Each day I get to ask, "Who am I being today?" I can feel and show up in the way that I want to.

This to me is true freedom, real self-expression, when I am no longer afraid to be seen and to love myself because of what others and the world may do in response. I cannot control all of that anyway. All I can ask myself is, "Was I me today?" If at the end of my life I can look back and say I was really me, I loved me, I felt so entirely connected at least more than half of the time, then I believe I will have lived well.

I look at my sisters-in-writing and ponder: What are the messages in our book that initially inspired us and, at times, still frustrate and overwhelm us? What can readers hear from each person in our circle?

I notice how Marna speaks to motherhood, and claiming her self-authority, self-care, and boundaries, while loving fiercely and bringing in immense compassion. I admire her willingness to ask for what she needs, naming the overwhelm, being radically honest, and calling us all to be with her in these spaces, encouraging permission for us all to be as we are and to step into well-being, too.

I see Deborah's grief and loss and the beauty of how this altered her world and calls forth her enormous, loving heart and her passion for community, music, and connection. Her complete and utter bravery to be with it all. She offers us the honor of being with her, permission to be with the depths of our shattering and still experience the full spectrum of shiny, joyful, connected moments.

I notice Owen calling us to love and celebrate life and who we are. Her finesse with being in the unknown, with dissonant feelings and parts of ourselves. Her willingness to be in the deep spaces of rage and despair, yet hold out hope, and to allow all of our parts to be and be loved. She gives us permission to celebrate, to fiercely allow the unknown, to have it all and love it all.

Maggie brings these hugely wonderful sparks of passion and truth. An artist at heart, finding such a range of expressions for those sparks of the divine. She has been with fear and rage and the depths of despair. She gives us all permission to bring out that inner fire. To burn brightly. To drop our masks. Permission to transform wildly into the beings we already are.

And to myself. Do I have any gifts? Am I enough? I ponder, can I claim this great story of mine? My body asks, is it safe? It is safe now, I tell her, and she becomes excited. She wants to claim these gifts and passions. Still some trepidation. Still some uneasy steps. It's so much easier to see it in others, and so much harder to see it in myself.

**Emotions the author experienced:**

Overwhelm, joy, hope, compassion, self-authority, well-being.

# EMOTIONAL CHECK-IN

What emotions do you feel about the process of healing old patterns and emotional stories stored within you?

Are there any wounds or patterns that you feel called to heal and transform in your life?

What permission slip could you give yourself to embrace healing and fully claim your magnificence and gifts?

# Permission to heal collective wounds

## Healing Collective Wounds

by Holly

I've been experiencing emotional turbulence and resistance to the life I am creating, with a ruminating fear of not having enough resources – time, energy, money, and so on. I am attempting to create a life where I thrive rather than just survive, and some days it seems like my entire inner world is against me. It's as though my body is terrified that if I follow my dreams I will die. But why? What is it that I need to notice, accept, honor, or release to feel aligned with living the life I desire?

I check in with my emotions:

Sadness, fear, and abandonment...

As I named my feelings, Maggie asked, "Is this yours, or collective?" The question struck like a lightning bolt.

These feelings are not just my wounds, they are also echoes of a collective struggle by my ancestors to survive the relentless grip of poverty. In a state of constant survival, where food and shelter today matter more than thriving in the long term. Doing whatever it takes to survive is more important than enjoying how you live long term, because you may not live very long anyway.

I have often found myself raging at the constant portrayal of mothers as all-loving, all-giving, fundamentally nurturing energies, as that has not been my experience. I was fascinated by mythological characters like the Greek Medusa and Indian Kali. So, when I stumbled upon emotional trauma specialist, Dr. Daniela Sieff, talking about the death mother archetype, there was a flood of relief. Finally, someone was explaining what I had known: mothering through poverty and extreme circumstances can lead to a mother's actions or feelings threatening her child's life or well-being.

It's not sadness I feel, it's a deep well of collective grief for the family members lost. My personal family, and our global family, too. I intuitively place a hand on my heart and say, "Aww." It helps me acknowledge my uncle, who died at age 14. Working on a boat wearing women's boots because he didn't have his own, he drowned when they filled with the oily water and held him down. My grandmother, who was brought up by an older sister after her mother died in childbirth, placing burdens on them both. My great grandmother, whose mother also died in childbirth. Many men and fathers lost to tuberculosis, with poverty contributing to its spread.

My eyes well up as the grief is felt. It sits heavy on my chest. I take a deep breath, and compassion rolls in. Hand still on heart, I imagine my ancestors gathered around me, and I say, "Thank you for showing me your grief and why you are worried I may die if I focus on joy and long-term goals." Their messages passed on in the memory of my cells. I bow to them with deep respect for how their lives led to my birth. I ask them, "If I have the courage to live a happier life than you, please will you bless me?" Celebration swells in my heart before I take a sharp breath in, as my mother's presence looms over me. I am frightened for my life and don't trust her.

I think of how many times my mother told me I was a burden to her. It was her truth, and I longed to be seen as a joy. I recall her words that still ring in my ears and burn my heart: "Never have children, because they just fuck off and leave you." Her own abandonment wounds passing on the hurt, instilling guilt in me for becoming an independent adult. I carried a toxic form of shame for wanting a life of my own, for attempting to have reasonable boundaries, and for the overwhelming inability to console my mother's grief and abandonment.

The thing with shame is, it's sticky. In challenging times there is this temptation to believe it. A habit of shaming myself out of who I am and how I want to be.

In my mind's eye, I see my mother's face and I say, "I'm grateful for everything you gave me. Your dependence on me was also too much. I am responsible for my part, and I leave your part with you. I am the Little One, and you are the Big One. You give, and I take. I give you a place in my heart." I hand back a rucksack, filled with the feelings of guilt, shame, and abandonment that weren't mine to carry. "What do I do with these?" she asks. "Feel into them," I reply.

My own sense of abandonment is now lurking: *Quick, quick, please her before we lose the love and feel worthless and unworthy again.* I thank the feelings of rejection and fear sitting in my belly and chest. Placing my arms across my shoulders in a self-hug, I tell my younger self, "It's okay, I'm here for you now. I've got you, you're safe. I'm here." My wise adult self nurtures the wounded part of me. My heart opens, acknowledging the desire for connection and the discernment of the need for healthy boundaries.

Sometimes I can feel the emotions arising, and by exploring the collective wound a greater sense of inner peace can be found. My own emotions are, after all, intertwined with the stories of my ancestors. It still amazes me how much we can sense what has gone on in a family, even when we don't know the full story. It plays out and is picked up so subtly. I am moving beyond the known experience of some of my more recent ancestors, yet distant, healing ancestors support me with reassurance and wisdom.

Love, I have come to learn, never expects you to owe someone for it. It doesn't bind you or obligate you against your will. What the parents don't heal, the children feel. Adults who don't take responsibility for their lives are adults in age, but not in character. They are wounded children walking around in adult bodies, having tantrums to get their needs met, unable to fully be with their own emotions or their children's.

This has been me, too. I have craved being saved in order to have my developmental needs met by others. *I don't want to be responsible for my choices*, says my Little One. *I want others outside of me to love me. I'm tired of having to be there for myself, and feeling so overwhelmed and alone.* It's a paradox that I had to save myself, and I am so glad that I did.

Healing, for me, is the restoration of wholeness. It's not about fixing something that is broken, because we are never truly broken. This illusion of brokenness is just that – an illusion. The word restoration contains the word "rest," and this is no coincidence. To heal is to rest in our wholeness, to realize that we are okay, acceptable, worthy, enough. That means accepting both the light and shadow stories of ourselves and our ancestors with equal gratitude. When we open our hearts to it all and still discern healthy boundaries, we cease passing on intergenerational wounds. We honor our parents and treat others as we would wish to be treated.

In particular, I am handing back shame for saying "No" to emotionally abusive behaviors and the perpetual crossing of clearly-spoken boundaries. I include myself in the golden rule, treating myself as I would like to see all treated. The experience of abuse, neglect, and co-dependency left me confused at times, forgetting that reciprocity and balance are necessary for safe relationships.

### Emotions the author experienced:

Grief, guilt, toxic shame, compassion, abandonment, thrill, relief, compassion, well-being, trust, self-authority, love, empowerment.

# EMOTIONAL CHECK-IN

What emotions do you feel around healing collective wounds, such as within your family, group culture, or nation?

Do you ever notice yourself feeling blame, shame, or guilt that doesn't belong to you? How does this impact your healing?

What permission slip could you give yourself to release the weight of inherited emotions and more deeply accept your wholeness?

# *Permission to have a courageous heart*

## A Courageous Conversation

*by Holly*

A heart full of feelings brings energy, growth, and release, supporting us to rest in our wholeness.

Courage-
The heart feelings

-ous
full of

Con-
with

verse -
changed

-ation
action, process, state, condition, or result.

A courageous conversation is to speak of the feelings filling our hearts. It takes courage to be a human being with all our vulnerable, scared, masked parts. That doesn't mean letting them flood out sideways or in ways that scare and hurt others. It means turning towards our feelings with a sense of curiosity and understanding what messages they bring to us, so that we might be able to communicate our needs.

A courageous conversation is any experience of a heart filled with emotions that leads to integration, connection, and unity within ourselves and with the world and universe around us.

In my life, I've so often desired change in the outside world: "If only they were different." "I need to make them think a certain thing about me." "I need to make them stop!" "They should have been there for me."

In many ways, I was not accepting reality. I imagine myself pointing a finger at God, as if to say, "Life is not supposed to be this way. C'mon, fix it." The reality is, we have very little control over others. They have a habit of annoyingly doing, being, thinking whatever they want.

How, then, do we navigate the complexities of accepting reality and getting our needs met? I've not found a perfect answer yet. It takes courage to make a choice and be accountable for the results, and to be loving and compassionate to ourselves in whatever happens.

It takes courage to be with all of your emotions, too. Accepting them without judgment was a particular challenge for me, especially with feelings like love and anger. One of the best techniques I have found for accepting my feelings is to thank them as I notice them: Thank you for being here, and for your desire to keep me safe and whole. If you pay attention, the sensations associated with your emotions might change in response.

Conversations contain the essence of our soul, or the mask of an image we want to project to others. For me, fear is at the root of both a heart full of emotions and also the conversations that make me want to curl up in a ball and hide. Sometimes that fear is of my own making, based in my personal victim story. Other times it is created from collective victim stories. Sometimes anger arises that is really a fear: I'm angry with a person, for example, because I fear something – perhaps being bad, having no value, being abandoned, not mattering, not being lovable or worthy. I feel fear, so the anger calls me to restore a sense of balance by including my own needs.

Courageous conversations can be just with yourself and your younger parts, with your masks or characters like your Inner Critic, or with imagined true selves of others. They can also be real-world conversations, though that usually happens after the inner process of feeling my feelings.

People often ask, "What do I do when I feel them?" as if they expect their feelings to disappear. The heart is meant to be full of flowing feelings. After you thank them for showing up, notice where they flow. When we thank our feelings without judgment or rejection, it helps us move towards them with more ease.

There is nothing more to do than notice them, name them, thank them, and allow your curiosity to follow them. It's when I am present to all of the feelings inside of me, taking care of myself, that suddenly I get to a new state. Sometimes that's when truly healing real-world conversations can occur. Sometimes it just lets me feel at ease without needing to say or do a thing.

**Emotions the author experienced:**

Fear, compassion, paradox, acceptance, gratitude, courage, relief, peace.

# EMOTIONAL CHECK-IN

What emotions do you experience around the idea of having a courageous conversation?

What is a courageous conversation you might have about your emotions or needs?

What permission slip could you give yourself to turn towards your courageous heart with curiosity and speak to your needs and desires?

# Permission to celebrate

**Choosing to Celebrate**
*by Owen*

Dear Reader,

How do you celebrate? Is it something saved for birthdays and holidays? Does it have a weight of importance, or do you have freedom?

Over the last three years of working together, we have grown our radar for celebrations! We celebrate the usual stuff, and alongside it the daily celebrations of our emotions. We celebrate the love and the joy we have come to be with more fluently and the rage and blame that show up. We choose our celebrations and often offer them to each other through the process of listening deeply.

I used to be ashamed of the constricting emotions that plagued me, and I certainly didn't celebrate them! Now I find myself in celebration when rage shows up. I allow the full experience of the emotion to flow its energy, igniting a fire and showing me the path to freedom!

The celebrations can be honored with oneself, but to be witnessed is a full-on party! In the witnessing and the safety of another's company, the sharp edges of rage can soften and the expression can be felt fully and released to hope and trust. The same can be said for celebrating well-being, love, and self-authority. In the company of another, it becomes amplified and can be fully expressed into joy, freedom, and thrill!!

During our emotional check-in on a recent weekly call, I found myself naming grief, pity, overwhelm, and sadness. What was revealed next was anger, resentment, and blame. The energy of naming these emotions in the safety of our call allowed me to shine brightly in my blame and fully experience it, not trying to change it or run from it or make it pretty. I was sitting in FUCKING blame!!

I began to smile and laugh as I felt into it, and the experience brought on the celebration. Celebrating all my younger parts who needed to be witnessed in their blame and recovering, to the nurturer who can hold the celebration of blame as I transitioned to compassion and love. YES, I am alive and kicking, and my emotions are celebrations of this aliveness.

I have also come to our calls and named love, joy, compassion, and passion, quickly skipping to name other emotions, only to have one of these courageous women slow me down to celebrate the love, joy, compassion, and passion, asking me to sit in the resonance of these emotions and stay. So often we rush to move through our most expansive emotions, missing the sweet elixir that we so need to feel.

To be witnessed in the range of your emotions is a celebration and an amplification of being. Little by little, we step into our wholeness with celebrations, moment to moment. The celebration is a choice.

# EMOTIONAL CHECK-IN

What emotions do you experience around celebrating the small and everyday moments in your life?

How often do you take time to celebrate the little wins in your day, and what holds you back from doing this more often?

What permission slip could you give yourself to embrace daily celebrations about yourself, even when they seem small or insignificant?

# Permission to be on a journey of becoming

**Pausing to Celebrate the Imperfect Journey**
*by Marna*

This morning, I am recalling the truth I landed in a few days ago:

I will never transcend anger or fear. I can't overcome these emotions once and for all. They are both a fact of life, a natural part of being a human in relationship with other humans, in an unpredictable world.

For so long, I've felt I was flawed for experiencing anger and fear. I've made myself wrong so often for feeling them because of how I react when I'm caught up in them – because I disconnect from myself and others when I desperately want to connect and show up from a place of calm, compassion, patience, and confidence. Self-blame and shame seem to keep hissing at me: *There you go again… Fear and anger make you weak and unworthy. You are wrong to feel them.*

I hadn't realized, until a few days ago, that all this time I was holding onto the belief: *If I can just master the skills to be more resilient, then I won't have to experience these emotions anymore!*

I notice compassion swirl in for that part of myself that was clinging to this directive and the deliverance it promised. My heart softens toward her … and I feel a softening into acceptance: *I will never transcend anger or fear.*

Sitting in this mix, I can feel a new realization taking root:

I don't *have* to transcend anger or fear.

I feel a mix of relief and excitement wash in, as I take in what this means…

If the goal isn't to rid myself of anger and fear altogether – and if I recognize that others feel these emotions too, and we are all perfectly normal humans for feeling them – then I don't have to be the perfect picture of calm!

Of course I will keep improving my self-regulation skills to ground myself in the moment – that's the sweet goal I'm aiming for – but I can also celebrate the progress I've already made!

While it's true that I still find myself frequently swept into arguments with my kids, or shutting down in overwhelm when faced with a decision or action that might disappoint others … I can recognize that it isn't happening as often.

The work I've done to notice and acknowledge my emotions and heal younger parts means that I'm not getting triggered as easily, not taking things as personally … that I AM sometimes remembering to breathe in the moment, remain calm, and stay present.

I can feel a part of me that immediately wants to minimize this progress, telling me *Sometimes isn't good enough*, pointing out all the times I've failed and caused suffering, and calling attention to the huge gap between me and where I want to be. But I am letting that part be for now.

I take a deep breath and notice tears prickle my eyes as I tell myself: "It is something! It's a big step forward!"

In this moment, I'm also recognizing that while I'm still practicing these self-regulation skills, I can lean into my recovery and repair skills. That's the real work I've been doing over these past years – and I can see what a triumph this is!

I want to celebrate!

I've made HUGE progress in my recovery and repair skills! There have been so many times, after I was caught up in anger, fear, or overwhelm, when I made time to allow my emotions to release, spent time with the part of myself who was feeling ashamed, and offered her compassion, grace, and love.

And I'm recognizing that this recovery process is often what has allowed me to access calm, compassion, and clarity so that I could repair my relationships and ask for what I need. Because repairing relationships is so important to me!

I know my past woundings have made this a passion spot for me. When I feel I have done wrong – like I've treated someone unfairly, disappointed them in some way, or disrespected their time or feelings – there's a part of me that feels desperate to repair the damage so they won't withdraw their approval of me. Over the years, this part has had me scrambling to apologize and make it up to them, along with many unhealthy people-pleasing strategies that have been mirrored back to me. I can see clearly what I do, and I am on the road to catching myself more often.

It's so easy to dwell on how imperfectly I make repairs, how many of my attempts *haven't* gone over well, or how many times I didn't put in the effort to repair … I can feel the shame just below the surface, wanting to pull me down...

But I want to celebrate that I take a stand for reconnecting! I am seeing that one of my graces is that I am deeply committed to restoring the integrity of my relationships.

The underlying message that I communicate each time I do attempt a repair, however imperfectly, is:

*This relationship really matters to me. YOU really matter to me. I made a mistake, and I'm sorry. I am committed to doing better next time.*

This urgent desire to reconnect has long had me leaning into the pain and discomfort of separation and growing the edges of my vulnerability, all in service of deeper connection. And I can see that this is what makes me the amazing mom, partner, coach, and human that I am.

Yes, I am still doing it all imperfectly. Yes, I will forever be a work in progress. And yes, that makes me deeply uncomfortable.

But today, I am noticing and acknowledging that as I continue to practice all of these skills, I am healing and my skills are getting stronger.

This is the work I am committed to keep doing.

For myself. With others.

*Keep going.*
*You're already doing it.*
*You're on the path.*
*Keep walking forward.*
*One step at a time.*
*Trust.*
*Trust.*

### Emotions the author experienced:

Shame, blame, desperation, worthlessness, despair, compassion, relief, excitement, hope, love, self-authority, passion, trust.

# EMOTIONAL CHECK-IN

What emotions come up for you when you consider celebrating that you're on a journey of reconnecting with yourself?

What comes up for you when you think about healing as an ongoing process of becoming, where mistakes and imperfection are part of being human?

What permission slip could support you on this journey of becoming?

# Permission to change the cultural narrative around emotions

**The Need to Feel and Be Responsible**

*by Holly*

It's coming toward the end of 2021, and this week is the buildup to COP26 – the 26th time that the Conference of the Parties (COP) to the United Nations Framework Convention on Climate Change (UNFCCC) has met to set targets to address climate change. Here in the UK, I listened to the Queen speak about taking care of our children, our grandchildren, and their children's children by taking action now. Are we really having the courageous conversations needed about the issues in our world? Or are we relegating our feelings to the shadows?

Will we collectively choose to claim our ability to act together as global citizens, to do what we can as guardians of nature, of our own families, of all life? I am feeling pessimistic on that front. The external world so often seems like a metaphorical mirror to our internal world. In our personal life, we often hesitate rather than heed early indicators, and only when life takes more serious twists do we embark on the initiation to transform our ways. Yet it is possible to take these steps with greater ease sooner.

I find myself, at times, in the powerlessness of despair and hopelessness. Raging against the systems that are slow to change. Falling into the less-than-ideal behavior of apathy. Like the turning of the Titanic, big ships have a big turning arc where small ships are more agile and maneuverable. If collectively our systems are like the Titanic, then by my estimations there is no avoiding the melting of the icebergs – unless, perhaps, there is massive, coordinated action from a lot of individuals coming together and tugging away for change. But not just me, alone.

Helplessness rolls in. What can I legitimately do that will make enough of an impact? It can feel at times like I have to make my own life harder while many will continue to reap the benefits of damaging actions. The rage is so deep, it's passive. Do any of us know what to do? Are we simply waiting for someone to come and save us, or will we find a way to ultimately save ourselves? The microcosm is a complete replica of the macrocosm, and vice versa.

We are collectively drowning in the numbness towards many big issues in our global societies. It's uncomfortable to really be present with the emotions, like that dark rage, the utter despair, the fear of what this all means for the future. Rage and anger are emotions that get labeled as "bad," and we hide them within us. It's not socially acceptable to be this vexed and provocative. We'll be mad and bad if we show this. And so, the apathy continues, and little changes. It takes courageous hearts coming together to step out from social norms that hold us in the inertia of what's come before.

Here we are, the United Nations making pledges, but what does any of it really mean? We're setting targets that each nation gets to choose, even if they don't deliver the conference goals. Those targets are voluntary. If they are not met, what will happen? Absolutely nothing. There are no consequences. If a child wanted to do something that damaged others in society, they'd be modeled proper ways to behave. This is not our approach to governments and transnational companies ruling our planet.

It's absolutely enraging that this pantomime is our so-called best. I am annoyed, frustrated, impatient for change. This passion is useful, those signals of pain and annoyance are there to generate energy, the fire of transformation and balance action. Why do so many of us sit here quietly with the dark rage, the apathy, dampening our flames? Is it because we don't know what action to take? Or is it perhaps that the feelings are so overwhelming, and we're unwilling to truly notice them in their full-blown glory?

I know I feel separate. How do I connect with others on this? Why are we not working better together on this? Perhaps we all just feel so alone, so helpless. Many days I'm just exhausted from work. Maybe that's you, too? Too tired, too busy, too distracted to act further as we attempt to keep the balance between long workdays, family lives, communities, and beyond. It's natural to be juggling all the energies in our life: inertia, action, and transcendence. It's just a question of how much we mix these things.

Our collective culture has taught us that it's improper to display such powerful and active emotions, and furthermore that the economy trumps the need to care, connect, be with, and face our deepest shadows. This inertia impedes the transformational energy of transcending systems that no longer serve the thriving of all life. We hide, ignore, numb out the collective grief, trading all the beauty of nature and life for toys. A house, a gadget, a car. Whatever your thing, it's a toy to pacify the apathy, grief, and despair. Wake up. Connect. Feel it. Please, we need to feel it all so we can accept it and move towards action! So this shift can become our norm.

The big questions in my life are: What will I pass on to the next generation? What are the vital parts of our culture that need to be maintained, taught, propagated? I believe that if people can fully feel all of their life experiences and know how to properly respond to them, then perhaps there is hope. Perhaps something can be done as they embrace their passions and take action. I want to fire that up – to move more of us towards meaningful lives, communities, and actions. That is why this book is evolving. It is the cultural perpetuity that some of us want to share and know is important.

The pit of my stomach is tense. This situation of hurting our planet and each other brings out feelings of anxiety within me. I'm okay with that. It should. Instead of fighting it, I thank it and move towards it with curiosity. I look at it, play with it, ask it what it's here to teach me. I celebrate it. Our planet will continue to burn up until the human virus is put out, adapts, and mends its ways. I'm called to release my negative stories about such feelings and experiences and, instead, approach everything in a celebratory way. This is what it means to be living your great life story: to release yourself from the seriousness and become deeply involved in the game of life.

As a friend reminds me that a lot of little tugboats can turn a big ship, hope floods in. My stomach unclenches a little. Feeling, being with, getting honest about this stuff is how we move forward. When I acknowledge the feelings, they loosen their grip and thank me for accepting them. Honoring those feelings is the start of change, both personal and collective. This is something to celebrate. I think of the process of transformation as an exciting show on a stage, a moment and experience to be delighted in and moved by. All shows need an audience. Our stories of pain, "stuckness," and greatness each need to be acknowledged and accepted by the audience.

On our world stage then, I am deeply moved by the courage, tenacity, and community I watch in the Black Lives Matter movement. I celebrate how trans people embrace difference and unintentionally challenge social norms by simply being. How those who have suffered sexual abuse recalibrate their nervous systems and reclaim their "enoughness." I rejoice in how the planet is pushing back on climate change to let us know something needs to shift. Nothing makes me more joyful than to see someone with lived experience of any form of wounding transcend the story of pain and reconnect with the power of personal and collective sovereignty. To not abandon oneself, or each other, in the face of genuine wounding, minimization, and marginalization.

Acknowledging the truth of suppression of any soul matters. You matter. They matter. Finding our commonality, similarity, what unifies us, matters. I encourage you to read Layla F. Saad's book, *Me and White Supremacy*, or Alok Vaid Menon's book, *Beyond the Gender Binary*, to explore this. Reading both, I came to recognize that anything I suppress in others is actually something I reject in myself.

In our role as the audience to this great play of life, our responsibility is to acknowledge each player's story, to allow their current truth to be, and to hold out hope for realization of the potential for greater liberation. To remain open to the coexistence of multiple realities, perspectives, and meanings, without the need to deny the others. To acknowledge pains, hurts, and suffering, without taking on undue shame, guilt, and blame. To feel it, and move through it, together, rather than avoiding the uncomfortable, messy, risky, utterly human feelings and thoughts. The greater our self-compassion, the greater our compassion for all others.

When wounds of any kind – planetary, collective, or individual – are looked upon, felt, viscerally experienced, it releases us. Wounding one wounds all, after all. Hurting our planet, nature, other communities, ultimately hurts ourselves in the long run. Allowing experiences of otherness, being treated as separate or less than, needs to be spoken about and then accepted by the audience. What we deny within ourselves, we deny within others. The shadow, after all, is not filled with scary monsters, but with the characters we wish to deny and avoid. Perhaps because we don't yet know how to offer these parts of us love, acceptance, and compassion.

Emotional suppression is a pattern that permeates a wide swath of issues. It's a pattern that needs healing. The cause must be known to resolve the effect. Some say feeling this stuff doesn't change anything. I say *not* feeling this stuff ensures transformation can't even begin. The genuine pain, the remorse, even shame needs to be felt and not carried in ways that come out sideways, so that compassion can be ushered in, responsibility taken where due, and healing can begin. It is one thing to discern what is unhealthy, harmful, undesirable and set healthy boundaries. It is another thing to judge. There are absolutely times when some people are so damaged and damaging that they're not open to witnessing another perspective, and permission to act in ways that restrain harm is very useful.

How can this harm to our planet, the very material that sustains and nurtures our lives, be restrained and stopped for the greater benefit?

As above, so below. Our governments and systems are but a reflection of what we tolerate, the standards we allow. I'm not out on marches, even though they matter. I don't want to risk being arrested, being around violence, looking improper. Is this really a deep fear, a sense of society abandoning me, labeling me a nut job or a hippie? I want to belong.

I am doing more than some. I trained people about sustainable construction. I have tried to work for ethical companies and organizations making a positive impact. It wasn't enough. They were half measures that didn't go far enough. The reason given: cost. Business is about making money. What is the matter with us? How is it acceptable to say this? Surely the purpose of business is to contribute to society in helpful, socially constructive ways. Surely worthy deeds create worth and monetary value. Or at least they should. Is the ecosystem primed to reward behaviors that aren't useful?

Yes, I know the reality that our system requires money. I'm not naive. It is naive to think that if you focus on the money, and not on contribution, it will make you successful. Maybe in the short term you get some extra toys. In the long term, we are going to wipe ourselves out with unsustainable behaviors. We will not save ourselves, because it was too expensive. Really?

It hasn't happened yet, though. Besides, global warming will mean nicer weather here in the UK; people will want to move here, we'll be richer. Will we? Really? They say true richness includes the wealth of health. Without our planet we won't have that.

Soc-I-ety needs to be balanced with a focus on comm**U**nity – shifting the focus from **I** to **you**. The litmus test for my decisions or choices is: "Would I want that impact to happen to me?" If not, then I won't let it happen to you. When we truly get clear, it becomes apparent that if I hurt you, it ultimately hurts me, and vice versa. This is the nature of physical life, too. It's like a perfect way to redress the balance, keep the score. The question is, can we transform and transcend before nature pushes us to?

Our collective focus right now is on reduction, doing less, moving away from what caused harm. It keeps us stuck in the paradigm of sameness. Innovation comes not from imagining what we don't want, but from imagining what we need to want. We need to create space to think in such radically different ways that the old ways are blown out of the water. Another pattern of our times: we focus on running away from and avoiding what we don't want to experience rather than launching towards our desired outcomes. We "manage risk" instead of dreaming new worlds into being.

I think that if more people in the world were having emotionally honest conversations, the world would be a better place. People would no longer make excuses for not speaking up. By speaking up, I mean expressing what they really think and feel about the ongoing events in our world, whether it be the environment, politics, injustices, inequalities. It is a diverse ecosystem that has resilience. By allowing many different perspectives, we create a more resilient culture and planet.

We need more people who are courageous enough to stand up for what they feel and speak out constructively and courageously, operating as whole beings, with no hint of being in their victimhood. Believing that they are worthy, that one person can make a difference when we come together in organized ways.

Can you imagine what a world full of people connecting like this would look like? What do you see?

### Emotions the author experienced:

Rage, pessimism, confusion, impatience, despair, hopelessness, numbness, pity, guilt, passion, overwhelm, worry, blame, optimism, passion, fear, love, self-authority, trust, freedom.

# EMOTIONAL CHECK-IN

What emotions do you experience when you reflect on global challenges like the environment, politics, or social issues?

How do you typically process or handle the emotions that come up for you when thinking about these challenges?

What permission slip could you give yourself to more fully acknowledge and accept these emotions and express the needs and desires they are calling you to notice?

# Who We Are and How We Got Here

Journeying to explore our emotions and witness each other through the emotional check-in process has allowed us to reflect on our personal and collective journeys. We are humbled and excited to share what's been true for us. Here are some reflections from each of us on what that was like. Thank you for witnessing us.

## Owen Sea Luckey

My journey to embracing my empathy, sensitivity, and intuition has been a winding path, marked by resilience and profound transformation. From a young age, I learned to stifle my emotions for fear of vulnerability. Yet, life spoke to me through pivotal moments – childbirth, a battle with cancer, personal loss, and the upheaval of the Covid-19 pandemic. Each event was a message from my body, urging me to acknowledge and heal.

Through years of exploration in therapy, bodywork, and diverse healing practices, I began to unravel inherited emotional patterns. This journey pushed me to deepen my spiritual practices and confront emotions I had long suppressed – notably, my capacity for RAGE.

As an artist and coach, I channel these experiences into reimagining dolls and garments, guiding clients to reinvent their lives authentically. Emotions now form the cornerstone of my work. Strengthening my emotional resilience has empowered both myself and those I serve to uncover authentic voices and reconnect with soul-nourishing passions.

Joining this collective to write our book, amid the chaos of the pandemic, was a transformative experience. Through courageous conversations and shared stories, we found solace and solidarity. In this community of powerful women, I felt safe to explore and reveal the depths of my soul.

The pieces I contributed to our book reflect my journey of embracing life's chaos, reclaiming my identity, and granting myself permission to feel deeply. They reveal a path toward healing and growth, illustrating my evolving relationship with emotions from a place of new-found strength and understanding.

As I continue navigating my emotional landscape and honoring the impact of my actions, I am profoundly grateful for this collective journey. Together, we harness the transformative power of embracing our emotions and bearing witness to each other's truths. Thank you for joining us on this remarkable voyage of self-discovery and empowerment.

## Marna Fujimoto-Pihl

I am a writer, creative soul, mom, and transformational coach, on a journey to reclaim self-trust, radical acceptance, and joyful responsibility.

My deep desire to be a better emotional guide and space holder – especially for my kids and my clients – is what led me here. At a young age, I learned to minimize and dismiss my emotions to meet others' expectations and get the connection and belonging I was looking for. This pattern followed me into adulthood, where the pressure to do and be "All the Things" had me constantly striving and putting my needs on the backburner … which led to frequent cycles of resentment, anxiety, guilt, overwhelm, and burnout.

My life's journey has challenged me to confront and heal this pattern. Motherhood, entrepreneurship, pandemic lockdowns, neurodivergence, and more have sent me on roller coaster rides of emotions I couldn't dismiss or ignore. These emotions were calling me to unearth, challenge, and unravel old stories and ways of operating that caused me suffering.

The years I've spent in this collective, sharing and writing about my emotional experiences, have been a wild and transformative journey. When we began our time together, I was struggling to parent two young kids amid a pandemic lockdown, without a support system or time and space for self-care. I was burnt out, carrying so much shame, and the armor I was using to hide my emotions was thin and fragile.

Feeling so emotionally exposed was deeply uncomfortable. Arriving on those calls to share and be witnessed in my emotional truth took a lot of courage, but when I did, I was received with compassion, tenderness, understanding, and love. These women held space for younger parts of myself who felt hurt, ashamed, and full of fear. They showed me I am accepted and loved no matter what, and gently helped me recognize and release stories of unworthiness.

The pieces in this book reflect my journey to acknowledge buried anger and reclaim my voice, dissolve shame and stories of unworthiness, embrace imperfection, and take responsibility for my own happiness, health, and well-being. I am still a work in progress, yet I have claimed more self-authority by giving myself what I want and need to thrive: deep connection with others, being in community, creating art and crafts, moving my body, seeking out delight, making music, and tending to my growing urban homestead.

A key part of my coaching work is partnering with clients to become more aware of, and practiced in, experiencing their emotions, so they can reclaim and express more of who they truly are. I am passionate about supporting people on their journey to explore and share the gift of their unique strengths, presence, voice, and experience. I am deeply grateful for this collective journey and for your decision to join us.

## Deborah Thornton

I'm a writer, singer, and transformational life coach whose personal journey includes seven decades of life, a richly varied career path, and cross-cultural experiences around the world.

My emotional journey began in the 1950s, when being a "nice girl" was the key to success in polite society. "Nice girls" don't get emotional (at least, not in public). My mother did her best to turn me into a "nice girl," and I did my best to earn her acceptance and praise. But no matter how hard I tried, my feelings and desires were either too much, or not enough. And if "nice girls" didn't want what I wanted or feel what I felt, then what kind of girl was I?? Fretting over that conundrum led to a strong sense of shame for not being loveable just as I was.

Anger was the biggest taboo of them all. Any infraction was sure to result in a one-way ticket to my room. That's not the full story, though. Exiled to my room, I knelt on the floor, bit the edge of my mattress, thought bloody thoughts, and screamed bloody murder. Clenching my jaws and pounding the mattress with my fists, I released wave upon wave of outrage until I collapsed in tearful exhaustion. Expressing that forbidden rage with all of my might was my secret, exhilarating revenge on my mother or anyone else who thought I would curtsy to the "nice girl" rules.

Fast forward many decades, and I'm a coach who helps people connect with the full spectrum of who they are, including their emotions. How in the world did I get here???

The shift began when I studied clinical social work in the late 1970s. Learning to help clients identify and express their emotions was a radical act, given my childhood taboos. Therapeutic techniques like pounding a pillow to release anger echoed and validated what I did instinctively as a child. Many years later, coach training took my understanding to powerful new levels as I learned to see emotions as "energy in motion" and to appreciate the shift that occurs when an emotion is fully experienced. A coaching course on emotional mastery helped me develop a deep, personal relationship with all of my emotions – including those I would rather avoid. My understanding and skills deepened further during the emotional resilience coaching program where I met the co-authors of this book.

This decades-long journey has given me a deep appreciation of the beautiful complexity of my emotional life. Learning to value the full spectrum of emotions made it possible for me to navigate the collapse of my marriage and the unfathomable loss of my beloved daughter in recent years. I don't know how I would have survived those tumultuous times without the ability to accept and release the torrent of emotions that came my way, over and over again.

How different my life would have been if I had learned all of this as a child, or even as a young adult! Looking back, I'm overcome with compassion for that confused and frustrated little girl – and for her mother, who was simply trying to teach her daughter how to be loved and accepted in the world as she understood it.

This new place feels liberating! Some emotions are still painful as hell. I'd be delighted if they never showed up again, but I'm no longer afraid of them. The feeling of shameful isolation has evolved into a rich kaleidoscope of emotions that bring color and meaning to my life. For that, I am grateful beyond measure.

## Holly McLoughlin

My emotional awakening has been a story of accepting my enoughness and realizing that I, like all humans, deserve to move out of survival-based living and into thriving.

Understanding the importance of my emotions and how they shape my life began in an unexpected place – my career as an engineer. At 26, I experienced what's sometimes known as the "dark night of the soul." My identity was crumbling and I was in the void before a new, more authentic identity had emerged. It was a deep low point where I was realizing that my thoughts had not been my own. I'd been a good girl, followed the culture's rules for success, and although I looked highly successful on the outside, on the inside I felt as though I was slowly dying, wasting my precious life.

I wanted to feel like I was daring to live my life in a way I enjoyed, being my authentic self, rather than masking up and merely surviving. One average work day, the senior bloke on the desk next to me said in passing, "Holly, when you get to my age, you never regret the things you did, only the things you never had the courage to do." His words sparked something in my soul. I knew in that moment that I needed to find the courage to do something else. I had no idea what would fulfill me, and I had no process to follow for figuring it out. Feeling hopelessness and despair, I knew no amount of external approval and professional success could fill the void inside me. I was constantly thinking, "There has got to be more to life than this."

I wanted to create a life that felt fulfilling and meaningful. I wanted to use more of my potential to make an impact on something greater than myself. And yet, there seemed to be an invisible barrier to me knowing what I wanted. Intuition was calling me, letting me know it was time to start listening to my inner guidance system.

Growing up, emotions had been something to fear or control. Coming from a chaotic background, I quickly learned to keep my feelings under lock and key; survival didn't leave room for vulnerability. As a result, I had spent much of my life pushing through to achieve, and numbing out how I felt. What I really needed to do was tune in to the guidance that my emotions were offering to me and listen to the messages they were whispering about my calling.

It wasn't until I began listening to my emotions – really listening – that the answers started to emerge. For so long, I had silenced my inner voice, mistaking it for a weakness. But in fact, my emotions held the key to my transformation. The more I learned to tune in to my feelings, the more I realized they weren't obstacles; they were my compass, pointing me toward a path aligned with my true self. Everything I didn't like experiencing was a call to explore what I did want to experience. My inner sensory system of body, thought, emotion, and energy guided me toward the practical outer life my soul truly desired.

In my coaching work now, I help others reconnect with that inner compass. We're taught to distrust our emotions, to view them as something to manage or fix. But what if emotions were the very thing guiding us toward a fuller, more impactful life? This realization was a turning point for me, and it's become the foundation of my coaching practice. Whether I'm working with clients one-on-one or leading group sessions, my focus is on helping people navigate their inner world so they can show up fully in their outer world – at work, in relationships, and within themselves.

For years, I ignored the parts of myself that didn't fit into the "successful" mold. But embracing the fullness of who I am – including the parts I used to hide – has allowed me to create a life and career that feel deeply aligned. Feeling our emotions allows us to relate with ourselves, our communities, and the planet in more beneficial ways. And that's what I offer to my clients: the permission to reconnect with their emotions, to trust in their own resilience, and to awaken to the power they've always had to create the career and life they really want.

Emotions are not the problem; they are the gateway to your true self. And that is where the real transformation begins. We can better understand our needs, desires, and what to let go of. When we start noticing and processing long-held emotions, then our dreams, goals, intentions, and creative expressions can truly flourish.

## Maggie Pierce

I am a life-long seeker, navigating the many facets of connecting emotions and their impact on the physical well-being of the body. I am a subtle energy worker, certified life, wellness, and professional coach, and a mother and grandmother. I am thrilled to be one of the co-authors of this book and to be by your side on this journey into emotions.

I cherish the wisdom that 20/20 hindsight can offer. In the comfort of the present, I can look back over my own life's journey to see the added wisdom that experiences have offered. I am now at a place that I could not have been without being full-on in the experiences, the hard places, the learning, and the wisdom life had to offer to me along the way. I am now at this place because of the dedication, tenacity, compassion, love, and acceptance this collective has held for our journey over these years together – not a journey we had to take alone. Our resilience was birthed out of our dedication to our personal and our collective longing to heal into a closer connection to wholeness.

The integration of working with and through my emotional landscape has been one of the many impactful tools for my toolbox. Some of the hard places are discussed in this book. Some of those hard places seemed even more dense because at the time I did not have the tools to accept my emotions and recognize what they could offer me, and perhaps to you as well. I hope that some of my experiences relate to your journey in a way that allows your emotions to launch you as energy in motion (e-motion) is intended.

I grew up in a small town in the Midwest. At the time, I did not understand the condensed version of myself that was becoming my foundation – mostly because I did not feel I fit in, and also because I thought I would outgrow this temporary setting. Try as I might to deny the cultural influence, the "walls" kept me tightly confined – especially emotionally. Looking back at that time with the wisdom of 20/20 hindsight, I realize my young self was stifled and denied her emotional expression. Lots of influences, like we all have, were holding back the strength of defining myself according to my inner gifts.

As was common in the generation that I grew up in, the parental style leaned heavily on punishment if someone seemed out of line ("Wait until your father gets home...," "Be seen and not heard," "Don't you dare act like that...," "Good girls don't do that..."). I felt the wrath of ancestral shame because I did not meet the standards of whoever was proclaimed as the authority – with church, parents, and teachers at the top of the list. Not having experience with feelings that could be nurtured and developed, I learned to assume the burden that I was at fault – I was not enough. I would consider my childhood a happy one for years to come – mostly because I didn't have the perspective or tools to recognize the true underlying hurt of discarded and misunderstood emotions. In living a life according to others, an energy of anger was building, though not ready to surface.

Years later, I met a consultant who spoke about courses she was taking to become a certified coach (there are no coincidences). Everything about coaching spoke to me – so much so that within a week, I was on a plane heading across the country to attend a sold-out course as my beginning steps to learn about coaching. My journey in coaching was first, and always will be, to know the journey within as personally "walked" and applied before any groundwork could be done to support others. This application of coaching was about to redefine my life and me. I was willing and open to change. Because of my passion to live a fully expressed life, I embraced the journey into coaching, as I watched my life grow exponentially. I aimed more toward self-love, self-compassion, and self-acceptance, while recognizing I had some shit to clear from previous times of misalignment and detours. Step by step, I was unfolding old patterns handed down to reveal myself in self-authority. I soon understood more of the courageous path each and every one of us is taking.

I have always had a quest for deeper understanding. As my coaching grew, so did my questions to uncover more processes and gems within my clients. I incorporated Voice Dialogue, Internal Family Systems, Great Story Coaching, Biofield Tuning, Root Cause Protocol, and Emotional Mastery into my coaching toolbox. I witnessed my clients having more strength, technique, and courage to respond to their lives and hold their own power. I have had the sacred honor of standing with each of my clients to witness their brave steps on their unique journey. I have had to take my own steps deep into the trenches at times in order to hold the strength and knowing for others. Life always has more to offer! I witnessed joy out of despair, thrill out of frustration and overwhelm, and so many passages for living because we were moving together with effective tools. Tapping into emotions became a valuable asset for my coaching.

I know our lives can feel overwhelming – even more so now, as the world is rapidly changing. I know we are all being called on some level to take time to heal. Sometimes looking back over life's landscape with new perspectives is the shift that propels the forward movement, equipped with new patterns. I believe that learning to accept and honor our emotions is one of the great steps toward being equipped to face the change the world is calling forth. I hope this book offers a path for you to explore the power of knowing and to feel equipped with the steps for honoring your unique emotions. I hope this book will be a source for your wisdom of remembering and experiencing the power of who you truly are on this masterful journey.

## Reflecting on Your Emotional Journey

Looking back across your emotional check-ins in this book, are there any emotions from the spectrum of emotions that you have never or rarely named? Could these be emotions you are uncomfortable feeling?

When you look back to your emotional starting point, has your ability to notice and name your emotions changed in any way?

What do you wish to celebrate about your emotional journey at this point?

# Closing Thoughts

We are deeply grateful for your decision to say "Yes" to yourself and this journey. We celebrate every new awareness, healing, and growth you've experienced so far.

We also want to emphasize that this journey is ongoing. It is our human right and a lifelong practice to intentionally engage with our emotions and be curious about the healing, growth, and expansion they point us to.

**We invite you into a culture shift where emotions are valued and honored.**

There is a deep longing and an urgent need to create a culture that normalizes emotions as an essential part of our humanity. This new culture is the antidote to isolation and shame.

**It's not about getting beyond our emotions** – it's about being in flow with them. It takes more energy to hold emotions at bay and numb out than to let their energy pass through.

**It's not about having fewer emotions** – it's about expanding our emotional spectrum so we can claim the full range of our human experience.

**It's not about feeling our emotions less intensely** – it's about harnessing their energetic gifts to move forward in life.

**It's not about hiding our emotions in the shadows** – it's about accepting emotions as part of our humanity and feeling safe to be witnessed when we express them.

**It's not about dumping our emotions onto others** – it's about noticing and processing them so we can communicate our reality in respectful ways.

**It's not about blaming or holding onto the past** – it's about recognizing and interrupting old patterns so we can be present to what is happening now.

**It's not about hiding our vulnerable inner parts** – it's about moving towards them with gentleness and curiosity, inviting them into the light of compassionate awareness.

**It's not about doing this alone** – it's about building communities and creating spaces that celebrate a healthy emotional culture. Spaces where we can be witnessed in our emotions without judgment, wrapped in unconditional positive regard and acceptance.

**We hope you will join us in co-creating this bold, new world!**

# Invitation to write a letter to yourself

Now that you've reached the end of this book, we invite you to write a letter to yourself using your nurturing voice. It could be to a younger part of you or to your current self.

This letter is your chance to connect deeply with your heart to offer compassion, encouragement, and any wisdom you've gained along the way. The permission slips you have written throughout the book will likely be a wonderful source of inspiration for this playful game of self-love. Let this be a space where you can celebrate your gifts, recognize how far you've come, and acknowledge all that you are becoming. There's no right or wrong way – simply allow the nurturing energy to flow from that sacred place within you.

You may find it easier to imagine what a great friend, loving person, or admirable person might say. As always, if writing isn't your preferred sensory approach, you could paint a picture for yourself, create some music or a playlist to nurture yourself, find some awesome videos online that make your inner self resonate with love and joy, or anything else you can think up. The most important outcome of this game is that when you read, look at, hear, taste, or smell this creation, you feel loved, enough, and uplifted.

Over to you, Dear Reader!

You can use this space for a letter to yourself:

# A Call to Community

Dear Reader,

As you close this book and open the next chapter of life, we want to extend an invitation to deepen the journey you've started here. You've been with us as the sixth member of our emotional resilience circle, witnessing the stories and reflections of others and exploring your own. Now we invite you to take the next step: to join a larger, growing community of courageous hearts.

We know that healing, growth, and emotional resiliency are not solo endeavors. We as humans thrive in the presence of a nurturing community that can model kinder and more useful ways of being with our emotions. The incredible power of sharing your emotions and adding your voice to a collective experience is that we all give each other parts of the maps we need on the way to realizing our wholeness.

As part of this journey, we invite you to anonymously share your most magnificent permission slip on our website (courageous-hearts.com). What is one permission you've given yourself during this experience? We would love to celebrate your courage in this. Maybe it's the permission to heal, to feel, to celebrate, or simply to be. By sharing, you'll be adding your voice to others who are travelling this way too. Together, we gain the courage to be vulnerable, more resilient, and more connected.

This is more than just a space for reflection – it's a growing community that reminds us we are never alone in our emotions. All emotions are our birthright, our way-showers, and our wisdom keepers.

Your contribution, no matter how small it may feel, is an important act of courage in shifting our emotional culture.

We look forward to continuing to expand the permission to feel, together.

With love and gratitude,

*Deborah, Holly, Maggie, Marna, and Owen*
The Courageous Hearts Collective

# *Permission to receive support on your journey from here*

Engaging with and learning from your emotions is a lifelong journey. You don't have to do it alone!

The following sections offer permission slips for understanding your emotions and resources to support you in exploring your emotional landscape.

# Permission Slips for Your Emotions

Emotions are part of our humanity, from the depths of despair to the expansiveness of love. Every emotion points us toward something that will help us be more connected to ourselves and others, express more of our unique essence, or claim more agency in our lives. In a sense, emotions operate like our own internal GPS.

We've included brief definitions here of key emotions for your reference. In some cases, emotions like blame, shame, and guilt can mask an emotion that we don't want to acknowledge. These "counterfeit" emotions are valid in their own right, but when we reach for them instead of experiencing a more "difficult" underlying emotion, we end up feeling separate from ourselves and others. Allowing ourselves to acknowledge and fully experience the underlying emotion will move us toward connection.

We've created a permission slip for each emotion to invite you into the experience and guide you toward the gift it offers.

## Hopelessness / Despair

Hopelessness and despair are intense feelings of hollowness and meaninglessness that arise when we feel insignificant, pointless, and helpless.

Surrendering to these feelings gives us time and space to turn inward and notice old, painful stories, seek a deeper truth, and claim our power to choose more helpful thoughts, words, and actions.

*Permission to accept what is painful and nurture yourself.*

## Worthlessness / Aloneness

A feeling of hollowness and insignificance that accompanies a belief that you don't matter, you aren't capable, and you don't deserve connection and belonging.

Notice how this feeling creates an intentional space to identify the thoughts that are telling you you're not worthy. Allow yourself to consider the idea that these thoughts are a lie, then seek out the facts that prove you are worthy. Reach out to trusted others to be witnessed with compassion, so your shame can begin to dissolve.

*Permission to open your tender heart to your innate value.*

# Loneliness

Loneliness is the perception of being alone and isolated. Sometimes there is a perception of being alone because we have a deep wound or challenge that feels too vulnerable to share.

Allowing yourself to feel loneliness invites you to notice your natural, human desire for connection and open your heart to receive love and compassion.

*Permission to desire connection.*

# Hatred / Violence / Revenge

Hatred is the intense feeling of hostility or dislike that is rooted in fear, anger, or injury. It mirrors something we can't "be with" in ourselves. Violence and revenge can also be experienced as a desire to hurt others in response.

Giving yourself a safe space to feel hatred, violence, and revenge invites you to notice your blind spots and recognize that the source of these feelings is within you, not outside. Bringing compassion to these places helps you to transform them by choosing more loving responses and boundaries.

*Permission to look at what you can't "be with" in yourself.*

## Rage / Apathy

Rage is intense, out-of-control anger or fury that comes when we feel invisible. Apathy arises when rage goes unprocessed, showing up as a numbness and futility (i.e., "What's the point?").

Giving yourself a safe space to express your rage allows you to notice what's being dismissed or ignored, and empowers you to take a stand for your truth, your voice, and the universal need for love and belonging.

*Permission to show yourself that you matter.*

## Blame

Blame is a counterfeit emotion that we reach for instead of anger. It keeps us from taking responsibility and healthy action.

Giving your blame an intentional space to complain or vent loudly relieves the pattern of hiding in rumination. It also lets you notice where you feel angry or powerless to set down responsibility for what's not yours, and take up responsibility and honor what is yours.

*Permission to explore your own responsibility.*

# Jealousy

Jealousy shows up when an aspect of a relationship feels threatened by another person.

Pay attention to the fear and anger that are showing you what's at stake of being lost in your relationship, so your true desires can be honored and you can set healthier boundaries to protect what is important to you.

*Permission to restore connection in your relationship.*

# Envy

Envy is the painful or resentful awareness of wanting to possess what someone else has, and feeling unworthy or unable to have it.

Pay attention to the fear and rage that are alerting you to a belief about what you can't have or won't experience. Then you can identify what you truly desire and explore actions to create what you want and need today.

*Permission to express your power to create what you need.*

# Hurt (Betrayal, Rejection, Abandonment, and Humiliation)

Hurt is the intensely painful feeling of separation that comes from an experience of betrayal, rejection, abandonment, or humiliation.

Acknowledging that you are feeling anguish, suffering, or distress from an emotional separation invites you to bring in compassion for those parts of yourself that desire healing.

*Permission to offer yourself compassion and forgiveness.*

# Fear

Fear is an unpleasant emotion we experience in anticipation of threat. At its core, it's a primal survival instinct. The work is to discern what's a real threat and what's perceived.

Allow yourself time to sit with your fear and notice what it's trying to alert you to, so you can choose to use the energy to take protective and nurturing action, or recognize that you're safe now to release the excess energy.

*Permission to protect yourself.*

## Anxiety

Anxiety is unease about a future outcome that's uncertain. It's made up of a combination of an alarm response and our thoughts.

Acknowledging your fear in the present allows you to explore what is a true threat and what is rooted in the past or future, so you can decide what is or isn't within your control and discern what action is really needed.

*Permission to discern what's present and true.*

## Angst

Angst is a persistent and unfocused insecurity or dread.

Allow yourself time to sit with your fear, and identify what specific expectations or outcomes you are attached to. Reflect on what is truly important to you, and trust yourself to take steps to make it real, releasing what's not in your control.

*Permission to identify and release expectations.*

## Anger and Fury

Anger is a natural response to a boundary being crossed. Fury is intense anger.

Acknowledging your anger and fury allows you to feel the emotion more fully and move the excess energy through you. Expressing your anger safely through yelling, throwing pillows, twisting a rag, swearing, or stomping (or even visualizing yourself doing one of those things) releases tension and creates grounded energy that you can use to speak your truth and ask for what you need.

*Permission to safely express your anger and restore your boundaries.*

## Resentment

Resentment is a counterfeit emotion that we reach for instead of anger. It keeps us from taking responsibility and healthy action.

Acknowledging that your feelings of indignation are justified allows you to be with the anger hiding underneath and let go of the story of powerlessness. Safely expressing the anger releases you from the pattern of rumination. It also channels your energy into speaking your truth and asking for what you need from a grounded and connected place.

*Permission to admit your truth and ask for what you need.*

# Pessimism

Pessimism is an expectation of a negative outcome. It shows up when you're uncertain about your ability to handle challenges in the moment or when you are striving to protect yourself from a risk of vulnerability.

Allow yourself to identify the true feelings underneath so that the drive to protect yourself loosens, and space opens up for you to trust your capacity to handle whatever happens.

*Permission to ease into hope and trust that you are safe to be vulnerable.*

# Guilt / Remorse

Guilt is a counterfeit emotion that we reach for when we have done something that's caused harm to another, yet we don't believe we have a right to feel anger or sadness.

We "take action" by making ourselves guilty, rather than taking responsibility and healthy action.

Allow yourself to sit with the true emotional response to your thoughts, feelings, and actions so that remorse can be felt. Then you can discern what wrong can be made right with clear, restorative action, and let go of feeling responsible for what you can't change or isn't yours.

*Permission to release over-responsibility and repair wrongs.*

## Sadness

Sadness points us to what we are missing in our lives.

Give yourself time and space to feel the depth of your sadness and acknowledge what you are missing. Notice where you can foster more connection in your life.

*Permission to call in connection and find a way forward.*

## Grief

Grief is a cluster of emotions that shows up when we lose something or someone important.

Gift yourself time, space, and compassion to be immersed in the emotions of your grief as they arise. Here you can gently acknowledge and process the magnitude of what was, honor your loss, and release what can no longer be. With time, you can welcome in deep gratitude and love to guide you forward on your journey.

*Permission to immerse yourself in the deepest experience of humanity and connect to your spirit.*

## Pity / Martyr

Pity and martyr are natural responses to a story of sorrow and suffering. They are counterfeit emotions that keep us from taking responsibility and healthy action. Pity shows up when we feel unworthy or powerless. Martyr rolls in when we feel responsible for too much or we feel angry and unable to ask for what we need.

Allow yourself to notice and feel the authentic emotions underneath the story. Then you can begin to acknowledge your desire for change and the actions within your control. From here, you can claim your power to choose your response.

*Permission to take responsibility to express your needs.*


## Crisis / Overwhelm

We reach for crisis and overwhelm to avoid feeling unworthy and powerless, but they are counterfeit emotions that keep us from taking responsibility and healthy action.

Notice your nervous system is feeling flooded, then slow down and feel the authentic emotions beneath the story you're telling yourself. This opens up space to examine the story and the expectations embedded within it. From there, you can decide what truly matters and take action to honor the choices that are right for you.

*Permission to slow down and choose what feels right.*

# Worry

Worry is anticipating what might or might not happen in the future.

Take time to hear what your worry wants to tell you, and thank it for bringing your attention to important information about the situation. Then, get curious about what is really true, and what action you can take that's within your control.

*Permission to anchor in the present moment and discern what is really needed.*

# Doubt

Doubt shows up when you have decided there will be a negative outcome.

Take time to hear what your doubt is saying and notice where you feel powerless to bring about positive change. Acknowledge and send compassion to any part of yourself that may be feeling rage, apathy, or hopelessness so the emotion can be expressed and moved through. Then you can assess what limitations are really true and which are perceived, and you can take stock of the resources you have and move into action.

*Permission to get curious about your truth versus perceived limitations.*

# Frustration

Frustration rolls in when our expectations are not being met.

Notice the feeling that things outside of your control are preventing you from achieving what you planned, and find a way to express and release the frustration and anger in a safe environment. Get curious about what expectations are present and why you are attached to them, so you can let them go, grieve the loss of what will not be, and set expectations based on what is.

*Permission to release expectations and take action from what is.*

# Confusion

Confusion is a mask for fear. It can show up as magnified states of indecision, stagnation, rumination, or numbness.

Allow yourself time to sit in the "not knowing" and "not doing," and let the underlying fear emerge to show you what is present. You can then ask yourself what is important and allow your instincts to guide you to what you want and need to do.

*Permission to rest and let the next steps be revealed.*

## Boredom

Boredom shows up when you are resisting a choice or change that can help you grow.

Challenge yourself to sit in the discomfort of your boredom, instead of numbing or distracting from it. Notice whether there is any fear, anger, or powerlessness getting in the way of making a choice, and allow yourself to express whatever is present. This allows you more freedom to take action and grow.

*Permission to take action in service of growth.*

## Impatience

Impatience is an agitation around expectations and outcome.

Notice the agitation of your impatience, and find a way to release the anger beneath it safely so you can pay attention to what is. Get curious about what expectations are present and why you are attached to them. This allows you the opportunity to define more realistic expectations and take action.

*Permission to let go of your attachment to expectations.*

## Well-being / Contentment / Satisfaction

The states of well-being, contentment, and satisfaction arise when we are living up to our own expectations and meeting our own goals.

Let yourself notice the feeling that all is well, as well as the sense of fulfillment and accomplishment. Expand this feeling by acknowledging and appreciating how you are making choices that reflect what's important to you and by recognizing you are enough.

*Permission to celebrate your "enoughness."*

## Optimism

Optimism is the assuring feeling of a positive outcome.

Notice the promise of a positive outcome, allow yourself to feel confident that you've created this, and eagerly anticipate the future.

*Permission to be excited about good things that are on their way.*

## Eagerness / Excitement / Enthusiasm / Thrill

Eagerness, excitement, enthusiasm, and thrill are varying degrees of anticipation of a positive outcome.

Notice the vibration of anticipation, and expand it by allowing your imagination to envision in rich detail what you'd like to have happen. Infuse your vision with the feeling of accomplishment so it can become even more real.

*Permission to celebrate and expand your feeling of possibility.*

## Hope / Trust

Hope is a deep desire for things to work out. Trust is a deep knowing that they will.

Notice your deep desire and expectation for things to work out. Allow yourself to become grounded in your conviction of a higher good and your faith in a larger force calling you forth to co-create it.

*Permission to be called forth into co-creating for the highest good.*

## Passion

Passion is an intense feeling of deep care and devotion.

Notice the burning fire of your commitment. Get curious about the ideal it upholds and what suffering from your past informs it. Give voice to your conviction to right the wrong in the world so you can honor this part of yourself and co-create for the higher good.

*Permission to speak your truth so you express your unique voice and share your gifts for the higher good.*

## Compassion

Compassion is a feeling of "being with" the suffering in yourself or another.

Notice the pain present in yourself or another, and allow your heart to open with empathy and understanding. Being with suffering is healing, and it nurtures your need to connect, belong, and know you matter, which ripples out to heal the collective.

*Permission to "be with" suffering to meet your human need of connection and belonging and to expand healing in the collective.*

## Happiness

Happiness is a state of bliss that arises when your needs are met.

Notice the sublime satisfaction and delight of meeting your needs, and allow yourself to celebrate taking responsibility for co-creating your life direction.

*Permission to feel the happiness flow into expansive joy and self-authority.*

# Love (Individuality, Joy, Self-Authority, and Freedom)

Love is a state of deep connection and recognition of your "enoughness," uniqueness, and personal power.

Allow yourself to revel in the freedom and expansion of experiencing unconditional love. Celebrate choosing to give yourself what you uniquely need and desire, as well as the power of expressing your essence in the world.

*Permission to bask in the unconditional love that calls you forth into authentic expression of your spirit.*

# Resources for Further Exploration

The following resources informed and inspired us as we co-created this book. We recommend them if you would like to deepen your learning as you explore your emotional landscape.

You'll find additional books, videos, and offerings at courageous-hearts.com.

## Emotional Fitness Toolkit

Developed by our mentors at Emotionally Fit Leaders, this was a key resource of the emotional resilience program that brought us together. Download it for free and begin to harness the power and wisdom of your emotions: emotionallyfitleaders.com/emotional-fitness-toolkit/

## Books

*Atlas of the Heart: Mapping Meaningful Connection and the Language of Human Experience*, Brené Brown, PhD, MSW. Random House, 2021.
   This study of emotions, through the lens of building connection, deepened our understanding of why we feel what we feel.

*Beyond the Gender Binary*, Alok Vaid-Menon. Penguin Random House, 2020.
   Alok's message of accepting all parts of yourself goes beyond the gender binary to offer heartfelt lessons for the soul.

*Bittersweet: How Sorrow and Longing Make Us Whole*, Susan Cain. Crown, 2022.
   We recommend this book for anyone looking to understand the essence of feeling bittersweetness and how it lives in their lives.

*Embracing Our Selves: The Voice Dialogue Manual*, Hal Stone, PhD, and Sidra Stone, PhD. New World Library, 1989.
> This groundbreaking book describes the Psychology of Selves and the Voice Dialogue process for communicating with and integrating the many different aspects of your inner self.

*Emotional Agility: Get Unstuck, Embrace Change, and Thrive in Work and Life*, Susan David, PhD. Avery, 2016.
> We recommend this book for anyone looking to create a road map of their emotions.

*Good Inside: A Guide to Becoming the Parent You Want to Be*, Dr. Becky Kennedy. Harper, 2022.
> We recommend this book to parents searching for a more compassionate, connected approach that releases self-blame and builds emotional resilience.

*I Know Why the Caged Bird Sings*, Maya Angelou. Random House, 2009.
> For those interested in emotional healing, this book offers insight into overcoming personal pain and finding strength in adversity.

*Insanely Gifted: Turn Your Demons into Creative Rocket Fuel*, Jamie Catto. Canongate Books, 2016.
> These games can help you become aware of and listen to your masked parts, better know your deepest instincts, and unlock your true power.

*Me and White Supremacy*, Layla F. Saad. Penguin Random House, 2020.
> This book will take you on a 28-day challenge to understand biases and privilege within yourself and create greater emotional awareness for action and change.

*No Bad Parts: Healing Trauma and Restoring Wholeness with the Internal Family Systems Model*, Richard C. Schwartz, PhD. Sounds True, 2021.
> This book will help you learn how to honor and communicate with every part of who you are and turn your parts into powerful allies for healing and growth.

*Permission to Feel: The Power of Emotional Intelligence to Achieve Well-Being and Success*, Marc Brackett, PhD. Celadon Books, 2020.
> This book was foundational to our understanding of emotional intelligence, the science supporting emotional release, and the process of emotional expression.

*Quiet: The Power of Introverts in a World That Can't Stop Talking*, Susan Cain. Crown, 2013.
> We recommend this book to anyone looking to understand and have their introvert qualities validated and normalized.

*The Black Girl's Guide to Healing Emotional Wounds*, Nijiama Smalls. Nvision Solutions, 2020.
> A valuable read for everyone in exploring disappointment, jealousy, rejection, low self-esteem, competition, overthinking, and family secrets.

*The Language of Emotions: What Your Feelings Are Trying to Tell You*, Karla McLaren. Sounds True, 2021.
> This book informed our collective understanding of what each emotion is trying to tell us and strategies for engaging with them as they arise.

*The Road Back to Me: Healing and Recovering from Co-Dependency, Addiction, Enabling, and Low Self-Esteem*, Lisa A. Romano. Lisa A. Romano Publishing, 2012.
> This book is a guide for those who may have experienced trauma, co-dependency, narcissistic abuse, emotional neglect, and abuse.

*The Shadow Effect: Illuminating the Hidden Power of Your True Self*, Deepak Chopra, Debbie Ford, and Marianne Williamson. HarperOne, 2011.
> This book is a comprehensive guide to understanding and harnessing the power of the dark side of our human nature.

## Oracle Card Decks

Archetype Cards, Carolyn Myss. Hay House, 2003.
 This deck will help you explore all parts of yourself and offers insightful ideas about the light and shadow aspects that need acceptance.

Kuan Yin Oracle, Alana Fairchild and Zeng Hao. Blue Light Publishing, 2021.
 These cards will guide you to a place of inner peace, inspired by the loving wisdom of Kuan Yin.

Work Your Light Oracle Cards, Rebecca Campbell and Danielle Noel. Hay House UK, 2018.
 These cards will help you tap your inner wisdom, align with your unique purpose, and weave the sacred back into your everyday life.

# Index by Author

**Marna Fujimoto-Pihl – The Sacred Space Holder**
Holding space with vulnerability and strength, Marna infused this book with the space to be with the messiness of our humanity and the gentleness of being.

| | |
|---|---|
| Diving in with Chaos | 25 |
| Forging a New Relationship with Fear | 33 |
| The Gift of Our Emotions | 39 |
| Developing a Nurturing Voice | 49 |
| All Parts of Us Matter! | 55 |
| The Imperfect Parent | 135 |
| Today I Showed Up for Myself | 169 |
| The Path from Anger to Self-Authority | 175 |
| Pausing to Celebrate the Imperfect Journey | 209 |

**Holly McLoughlin – The Keeper of the Dreamfire**
Dreaming this book into being, Holly brought us together with the idea of curating a set of courageous conversations about the power of our emotional wisdom.

| | |
|---|---|
| Breaking the Mold: Embracing Emotion as the New Norm | 17 |
| The Inner Nurturer is So Much More than a Nurturing Voice | 50 |
| Celebrating Yourself: Feeling Your Way from Victim to Vitality | 63 |
| Dare to Live | 71 |
| My Journey through the Mother Wound | 73 |
| Acceptance and Shame | 120 |
| Choose Love | 147 |
| Fill Up Your Love Cup | 150 |
| Responsibility | 163 |

| | |
|---|---|
| Claiming our Magnificence | 191 |
| Healing Collective Wounds | 195 |
| A Courageous Conversation | 201 |
| The Need to Feel and Be Responsible | 215 |

**Owen Sea Luckey – The Creative Yin Master**
Keeper of the book's flow, Owen held us in the rich weaving of layers, receptivity to the spiral of intuition, and mystical integration of the creative way.

| | |
|---|---|
| Emotions Matter | 1 |
| Reflections on Chaos | 30 |
| The Gifts of Emotions | 42 |
| The Nurturing Voice | 45 |
| My Victim Travels with Me | 57 |
| My Shattered Heart | 88 |
| Response to Maggie's Concealer | 99 |
| Naked on the Page | 100 |
| RAGE. HOPE. LOVE. | 105 |
| Sadness | 115 |
| Shame | 119 |
| School | 129 |
| Motherhood | 140 |
| Love | 148 |
| Responding to Maggie | 157 |
| Claiming My Voice | 166 |
| Covid Loneliness | 179 |
| Choosing to Celebrate | 205 |

**Maggie Pierce – The Resonance Keeper**
Guardian of the book's energy, Maggie kept us attuned to the resonance of the book, ensuring that our pieces vibrate harmoniously and land powerfully.

| | |
|---|---:|
| Untangling the True Nurturing Voice from Misinformed Beliefs | 47 |
| Staying Ashamed Keeps Me Locked in Shame | 58 |
| No Amount of Concealer Can Hide You from the World | 93 |
| It Only Takes a Moment to Destroy a Lifetime of Building | 107 |
| Rage that Takes Us Down | 111 |
| Sweaty Palms | 153 |
| Facing the Darkness | 185 |
| Patterns Stuck Within Us | 189 |

**Deborah Thornton – The Diamond Diva**
Master editor and full-spectrum soul guide, Deborah has helped us better express the gems in our words and trust in the deep river of the soul for this book.

| | |
|---|---:|
| Ode to Chaos | 29 |
| Shattering: My Journey through Grief | 81 |
| Mercy, Mercy, Mercy | 159 |
| A Letter from My Soul | 183 |

www.ingramcontent.com/pod-product-compliance
Lightning Source LLC
Chambersburg PA
CBHW072048110526
44590CB00018B/3082